BECOMING A MORE STRATEGIC PRODUCT MANAGER

Nine Lessons, Nine Days

Todd Birzer

Todd Birzer
Visit my website at www.kevolve.com
For any inquiries regarding this book, please email todd@kevolve.com

Kevolve Product Management

CONTENTS

INTRODUCTION: BECOMING A MORE STRATEGIC PRODUCT MANAGER

As product managers, we want to go big—we want to make our customers grin, and our competitors sweat. We want growth (preferably rapid) and we want profit. We want to make an impact on our company, we want to craft a powerful product portfolio, we want to punch back at our competitors.

No product manager wants to be a caretaker, no one wants to move the pawns forward one space at a time, no one wants to merely keep the lights on. Babysitting a product is not what we signed up for. And yet, for too many of us, we end up in this cul-de-sac.

Product management, by design, is hands-on. We want to dive into the details, get our hands dirty, be part of the daily push and pull. Our jobs should be a very tactical, we are not ivory tower theorists.

The problem is that we, as product managers, lose our balance. We let our tactical work smother the more strategic parts of our job, limiting our impact. Customers never see our breakthrough products because we don't create breakthroughs. Competitors never quite feel our punch. Our managers see lackluster revenue and profit growth. We let the tactical overwhelm the strategic.

The goal of this book is to help you become a more strategic product manager—to step away from the highly tactical, and step into the elements of your job that have a long-range impact on your company and its product portfolio. The goal of this book is to help you delight your customers, knock back your competitors, and deliver mouth-watering profits. The goal of this book is to help you go big.

STRUCTURE OF THIS BOOK

This book is set up in a series of nine lessons over nine days. In our Day 1 discussion, let's reorient ourselves toward—the often underinvested—strategic parts of our job. And we'll talk through the non-core tactical areas of our work that we should gracefully shed.

From Day 2 through Day 8, we'll focus on those areas of our jobs that we should lean into for maximum impact, those areas that we should say an emphatic "yes" to.

Finally, on Day 9, we'll look at the full package. If this were a cookbook, Day 9 would be the recipe—the practical steps you can take over the next three, six, and nine months to make your customers smile, lengthen your competitive lead, and generate healthy growth. We will also talk about the characteristics of excellent product managers—how we lead, how we influence, how we manage our time, and how we steer our work for maximum impact.

Along the way, we'll be looking at real company examples. We'll talk through companies that you likely know (LinkedIn, Google, Udemy), and some companies that you may not know (KeepTruckin, Nauto, Ancestry).

Nine lessons, nine days. You won't find product management excellence in nine days of learning. However, my hope is that nine days of learning, plus nine months of practice will get you there.

DAY 1: BALANCING THE STRATEGIC AND TACTICAL

A Gentle "No" and an Emphatic "Yes"

"Reactive product management," is how one product manager, based in Sweden, described it to me. The ingredients for product breakthroughs were all there—a growing market, a talented and innovative engineering team, and skilled product managers. And yet, more than 90% of product development work at this company was sales-driven, focused on minor enhancements to a push a particular deal over the line. The product managers were spending most of their time arbitrating, consolidating, streamlining and refining these requests. The team could find little time for customer interviews, strategy development, or exploring new product concepts with their development team. "We are hitting the wall. We can never seem to catch up."

I wish I could report that this type of situation is rare. Unfortunately, for many of us product managers, this is a picture of our days. We get pressed to solve a technical issue on our product, we spend hours in meetings coordinating complex projects, and we work through a lengthy list of requests from a key client. Research with customers gets pushed to next month or maybe next quarter. Competitive analysis is a once-in-a-while, haphazard task. We don't spend enough time with our engineering team exploring new possibilities, uncovering breakthroughs—innovating.

It's our common problem as product managers; we let the tactical overwhelm the strategic.

The good news is that this is all correctable. As product managers, we are gifted with positions of influence. We can set future product direction, we can guide development teams to create market-leading products, we can creatively seek growth. We can explore, innovate, and solve customer problems. We can create profits and competitive advantage. We can get runs on the board.

With focus and dedication, we can do all of this. But it requires us to find a healthier balance between the strategic and tactical.

When we, as product managers, do this—when we are smartly hands-on but lean strategic—we can have near-immediate impact. Excellent product managers, starting in a new role or re-energizing a current role, can find early wins in three months. We can reorient a product direction toward customer delight and competitive advantage within six months. By nine months, we can have a product (and product team) firmly on a path toward growth, market share gains, and healthy profitability.

Balancing the strategic and tactical elements of our work is the theme of our Day 1 discussion. We'll focus on four topics: our work as product managers; why we become tactical; those parts of our work that we should say a gentle "no" to; and all those more impactful areas that we should say an emphatic "yes" to.

OUR WORK AS PRODUCT MANAGERS

Let's start by looking at the full work of product management.

If you are a product manager today, I don't need to tell you that product management covers a lot of ground. Figure 1.1 outlines the work of product management, broken into four, interconnected and concurrent parts.

The work of product management	
Market intelligence	Market Customer Competition
Strategy	Strategy development
New product development	Prioritization Discovery and delivery Launch
Lifecycle management	Positioning Pricing Sales support Sales channels Product support Finding growth Obsolescence

Figure 1.1: The work of product management

Market intelligence: A strong understanding of market dynamics, customer needs, and competitive trends is a foundational element of product management. All our other work as product managers depends on an analytical and intuitive understanding of markets, customers, and competition.

Strategy: As product managers, we need a well-honed strategy to guide our decisions around long-term development priorities, positioning, pricing, and finding areas of growth.

New product development: A key aspect of our product management work is guiding and shaping a future product portfolio. We work with engineers and other members of our extended teams to create products with high customer value and competitive advantage. We do this by setting top-level development priorities, going through a discovery and delivery process with our engineers and user experience designers, and then launching these products out into the market with splash and promotion.

Lifecycle management: For products in the market today, we have many things to do—including positioning, pricing, supporting our sales teams, determining sales channels, working through product issues, finding growth opportunities, and (at some point) obsoleting our products. This area of product management is also called product marketing—and it may or may not be part of your job.

To put this all into one sentence: As product managers, we manage the full lifecycle of products and services to create exceptional customer value, generate a long-term competitive advantage, and deliver year-after-year profitability. This is why we come to work every day, this is our core purpose as product managers.

WHY WE BECOME TACTICAL

To delight our customers, smack our competitors, and create enviable profits, we need to focus our work on the areas of highest impact. In other words, we need to be more strategic. Let's look at why, despite all our best intentions, we get engrossed in the tactical elements of our job and underinvest in the strategic.

Where We Come From

We know, from research and experience, that product managers come from many different places. Think about your path. You may have worked as an engineer or part of a research and development (R&D) group. You may have been a product owner on a scrum team, or potentially a program or project manager. You may have come from marketing or sales, you may have worked for a client services team or in technical support. Maybe you just completed your MBA. These are all viable and valuable paths to enter product management.

Now pair this with the broad spectrum of work we do as product managers. Almost no one entering product management for the first time has all the skills they need.

If you come from a marketing or sales team, you may know how to analyze customer needs, but probably don't know how to work with an engineering team to steer new product development. If you come from engineering, you may have a good grasp of hardware or software development, but you probably know very little about segmentation, sizing, positioning, and pricing.

And very few of us—new to product management—can develop an effective strategy for our products, no matter what our background is.

The broad spectrum of product management work—market intelligence, strategy, new product development, lifecycle management—paired with skill gaps for newly minted product managers gives us the first reason we become very tactical.

The job, at first, can be overwhelming. We don't quite know where to start. We are, however, getting lots of requests, and as good corporate citizens, we dive in. We have a large deal in Germany, and our sales team has asked us for help. We set our alarms early and join teleconferences with our European group. We have a technical issue with our products and the client services, technical support and engineering teams are not working well together. Our managers have asked us to solve this. We get many requests for help, and we step in.

A second reason we get pulled into the tactical has to do with our personalities and skills. If you are attracted to product management, you probably enjoy working between and among different groups—

engineering, finance, marketing, sales, customers, etc. You probably also have experience managing projects. And you have product knowledge. This all makes you a prime candidate to lead product-related, problem-solving projects.

While each project may make sense, the sum is that we crowd our days with the tactical, leaving little time for the more strategic elements of our work.

I've worked with many product management teams and find product managers spend large amounts of time on product issues, sales support, and program management.

On the other hand, very few product managers spend enough time on market intelligence. We don't invest in interviewing and observing our target customers and lack a gut-level, intuitive understanding of customer needs. It's rare for product managers to have a well-honed product strategy we are operating against because we haven't spent the time doing this. And we don't do enough prototyping and experimentation in our new product development efforts.

These more strategic elements of our jobs as product managers are incredibly valuable—they help us guide our product portfolio for customer delight, competitive advantage, and sustainable profits.

But they take time, and if we spend our entire day solving product and sales issues, we won't get there.

SELECTIVELY SAYING "NO"

Being strategic takes time, and with a full workload, we need to get something off your plate to make room. We need to find areas of your job that you should say a gentle "no."

Let's start by looking at our "special sauce" as product managers. What is unique about our work as product managers? What makes us especially valuable to our organizations? I'll suggest four areas:

- We have a deep analytical and intuitive understanding of our customers and markets
- We are infused with our product vision and strategy
- We know how to steer product development toward customer delight and competitive advantage
- We are passionate about customer success

While others in the company may have parts of these, few other roles outside of product management (and executive management) have the full package.

Prime candidates to say a gentle "no" to are those tactical areas that don't require our customer, strategy, and product development expertise— in other words, those areas that don't require our special sauce.

Let's start by considering what you worked on in the past two weeks. Jot down everything you did, and then separate these actions into three buckets: strategic, tactical (core), and tactical (non-core). See Figure 1.2.

For the strategic bucket, include those areas that set you up for long-term impact: market, customer, and competitive analysis; strategy development; prioritizing development efforts; pricing analysis; and finding the best paths to growth.

Break up your tactical work into two buckets: core and non-core. For the tactical (core) bucket, include the day-to-day tactical jobs that require your product management "special sauce."

Product managers often spend large amounts of time working with development teams to refine and hone products before launch, and adjusting them based on customer and market feedback after launch. This work can be highly tactical, but it is also critical, and in sync with your role as a product manager. Additional examples include ongoing competitive monitoring, launch planning, pricing implementation, and product obsolescence. These are jobs that you, as a product manager, are uniquely qualified to do.

For the tactical (non-core) bucket, list all the tactical jobs that don't require your special sauce as a product manager. There may be many people in the organization that can do these jobs, you are just a convenient choice.

What did you do over the past two weeks?			
Area	**Description**	**Examples**	**Your actions**
Strategic	Strategic elements of your product management work	Market, customer and competitive analysis, strategy development, prioritizing development efforts, pricing, finding growth for your products	*List your actions here*
Tactical core	Core to your job and requiring a product manager's "special sauce"	Competitive monitoring, working with our development teams to define new products and features, launch planning, pricing implementation, product obsolescence	*List your actions here*
Tactical non-core	Non-core to your job and not requiring a product manager's unique skills and perspective	Program and project management, technical support, extensive sales support	*List your actions here*

Figure 1.2: Jobs over the past two weeks

In this last bucket—tactical (non-core) —are prime candidates to say a gentle "no" to. From my work with many product management teams, in a variety of businesses, I'll recommend three "no" candidates.

Program and Project Management

As product managers, we are systematic, organized, and motivated. We are very good at coordinating diverse teams to drive a project from idea to completion. Many of us have previous program and project management experience. Our managers find it tempting—and we are tempted ourselves—to step into program and project management roles related to our product.

These roles, however, are time consuming and don't require our special sauce as product managers. In most organizations, there are many people with excellent program management skills. Program and project managers don't need a deep understanding of customers, and they don't need to be steeped in product strategy. This job does not require our unique value as product managers.

Recommendation: Say a gentle "no" to program and project management roles. Consult with your team and politely pass this work to someone else.

Product Support

Another area of tactical danger for product managers is product support. We know our products inside and out, we've used them, dissected them, and prodded and pulled them. With this knowledge, we let ourselves drift into technical support roles. A customer calls a technical support agent for a product issue. Your technical support groups haven't done their homework, and don't fully understand the product yet. They take a shortcut and call you.

Recommendation: Get your support channels trained, prepared, and self-sufficient. When they have difficult technical issues, they should escalate these directly to your engineering team, without you, the product manager, being part of the support path.

As product managers, we want to know about top support issues. We own our product gaps and want to resolve underlying systematic issues. However, we don't want to be the person solving issues on a client-by-client basis.

Sales Support

As a product manager, you are an expert in your product area, and you may be very good in sales situations with potential customers. Your sales team may ask you for help, especially for new products.

Recommendation: Train your sales team and channel partners to effectively position, demo, and sell your product. Get them the right sales tools. Join them on some of their sales calls so that you have firsthand experience and feedback. But say "no" to more extensive help, like doing a roadshow where you demo a new product to thirty different prospects.

Opportunity Cost

Note that none of these areas—program management, product support, sales support—are wrong. You won't end up in product management purgatory for doing them. Your manager won't give you time-out and make you stand in the corner with your nose up against the wall. You aren't stretching the moral fiber of the universe.

This is all about opportunity cost. If you take on non-core tactical roles, you will have less time to focus on the more strategic areas of your job, limiting your impact.

How to Say "No"

Saying "no" is tough. As product managers, we don't have organizational authority to make unilateral decisions. Many executives have ill-formed ideas of a product manager's role and may place misdirected expectations on you. Many teams are also short-staffed, and product managers become the catchall, go-to team members.

My advice is to quietly and diplomatically work with your extended team, using all your political savvy. As you work through the nine days of this book, find a visible, impactful project to pursue, for example, a new discovery and delivery development process. Share the importance of this project, and let your team know that you need to pass along some of your current work to make time to focus on this new area. Recommend potential candidates for this work and see if you can gain agreement on a transition. Gradually step back.

SAYING "YES"

Saying "no" will enable you to say "yes." There are areas of your work to which you should say an emphatic "yes"—the areas you should lean into for maximum impact. These are the areas that, taken collectively, will enable you to create breakthrough, market-leading products. They will help you find growth in revenue, profit, and market share. They will earn you high-fives from your customers. They will leave your competitors quietly muttering.

Here is the punch list:

Customer Analysis

A deep understanding of our customers is a foundation for excellent product management. We need to sit down with our customers (and competitors' customers) and hear their stories. We need to know what motivates them, what problems they are trying to solve, what opportunities they are seeking. We need to study, to use Amazon CEO and founder Jeff Bezos' words, "the many anecdotes rather than only the averages."

The focus is on depth. Depth of customer understanding won't make you strategic, but you can't be strategic without it.

Competitive Analysis

One of our primary tasks as product managers is to develop a long-term competitive advantage. Underpinning this is a thorough understanding of our direct competitors—their strategies, their technology, and their next moves.

Beyond direct competitors, we need to recognize and prepare for disruptive technology. Too many companies overlook and underplay changes in the market that allow customers to meet their needs in fundamentally new ways. With eyes wide open we need to see disruptive technologies, both the opportunities and threats.

Strategy

A well-refined product strategy paves the way for long-term market success, but most of us product managers spend too little time here. This work includes vision, objectives, and strategy.

We need a product vision that articulates how the world will be a better place if we succeed. We need specific, measurable objectives to track progress against our vision. And to succeed with our vision, we need a product strategy.

Our product strategy should define our market arena, determine how we will develop the capabilities we need to succeed, pinpoint our competitive advantages, and articulate how we'll make money.

Prioritization and Roadmapping

Technology companies, and their product managers, often run into trouble with development priorities. They get sidetracked by a myriad of client requests; they get stuck in their bureaucracy; they let their product direction wobble. Product development becomes painful for these companies, and they struggle to release market-leading, breakthrough products.

As product managers, we can bring huge value here. We can set up a series of quarterly objectives and key results (OKRs), simultaneously directing and empowering product teams. We can use development buckets—a simple tool to focus our engineering efforts on those areas with the greatest impact.

Roadmaps, as a tool for us product managers, have both power and danger. When used correctly, they can help visualize and communicate a product strategy, and force healthy tradeoffs.

Prioritizing development efforts is one of the fastest ways we, as product managers, can have a big impact.

Discovery and Delivery

Our product enhancement ideas run the spectrum from excellent to utterly worthless. The trick is to enact a fast and low-cost process for separating the trash from those ideas that have strong market fit. A well-run discovery and delivery process helps us get there, giving us a tool for fast product evolution.

Discovery and delivery is best driven by a small, empowered team—typically a product manager (you), a user experience (UX) designer, and an engineering lead. Prototyping, experimentation, and rapid customer feedback are all part of this process.

Pricing

Systematic pricing analysis can have an enormous impact on a company's profitability. In fact, intelligent price changes can be one of the fastest and most effective ways to increase margins.

Unfortunately, most of us product managers do the bare minimum with pricing and leave it at that. We critically underinvest in this area.

Finding Growth

Generating revenue, profit, and share growth is a central job of product management. Many long-established products have strong growth potential, although this opportunity is often overlooked.

Our approach for finding growth varies through the product lifecycle— playing offense in the growth stages and playing defense in the mature and declining phases. We can also learn from the creative growth-hacking techniques of software startups, with little or no money for traditional, advertising-oriented, outbound marketing.

In our Day 2 through Day 8 discussions, we'll dive deeply into each of these "yes" areas, with examples and practical advice. In Day 9, we'll pull the whole package together, and talk about the three-quarter (nine month) recipe for finding excellence, for becoming a more strategic product manager.

DAY 1 FINAL WORDS

As product managers, we overinvest in the tactical elements of our job and underinvest in the strategic elements. Our job, by its very nature, should be hands-on and tactical. We want to be an active part of the daily push and pull. The problem is that we let the tactical absorb every working hour, leaving little time for those parts of our job with long-term impact.

If we want to have a substantial impact on our company and our products, then we need to create space for the more strategic parts of our job. We need to say "no" to tactical work that doesn't require our product management special sauce. And we need to say "yes" to those areas of our work that create product and market breakthroughs.

We'll start, as we should, with customers.

DAY 1 ON ONE PAGE

1. As product managers, we often let tactical work smother the more strategic elements of our job, **limiting our impact**. To create breakthrough products and generate strong growth, we need a healthier balance.

2. Our work as product managers covers a **huge breadth**—spanning market intelligence, strategy, new product development, and lifecycle management. Most of us, new to product management, have solid skills in some areas, but gaps in other areas. This combination of skills and gaps is completely normal and expected, but it leads us to be more tactical and less strategic than we should be.

3. To make time for the more strategic, impactful elements of our work, we need to **say a gentle "no"** to some of the less-central tactical work. Potential "no" areas include: program and project management, extensive sales support, and front-line product support.

4. After we shed some of our tactical work, we need to **say an emphatic "yes"** to the more strategic parts of our job. We need to spend more time with customer analysis, competitive analysis, product strategy, prioritization of development work, discovery and delivery development processes, pricing, and finding growth.

DAY 2: CUSTOMER ANALYSIS

Beautifully, Wonderfully Dissatisfied

In his 2017 letter to shareholders, Jeff Bezos, CEO and founder of Amazon, wrote that a "remarkable customer journey starts with heart, intuition, curiosity, play, guts, taste." He noted that "good inventors and designers deeply understand their customers. They spend tremendous energy developing that intuition. They study and understand many anecdotes rather than only the averages you find on a survey."

As product managers, this is us. A deep analytical and intuitive understanding of our customers is a foundational element of product management. To create excellent products for our customers—to create a remarkable customer journey—we need to approach our work of understanding customers with intensity, openness, and deep passion. A gut-level understanding of our customers won't make us strategic, but we can't be strategic without it.

Customers are trying to solve an issue, realize an opportunity, avoid a pain, and seek a gain. They are trying to satisfy their needs. As product managers, we need a deep appreciation of this. Our goal is to develop an intuitive understanding of the articulated and unarticulated needs of our customers.

We want to know the answers to a series of questions:
- What are our customers trying to do?
- What pains are they looking to avoid?
- What gains are they seeking?

- How are they solving for these pains and gains today?
- What's working and what's not working?
- What changes would they like to see?

And underlying these questions is a series of "whys." Why is this important? Why is this motivating? We want to get to the heart of what customers need, far beyond what they are asking for. Teasing out underlying motivations is a critical part of what we do.

Let's consider the words of Jeff Bezos one more time: "Customers are always beautifully, wonderfully dissatisfied, even when they report being happy and business is great. Even when they don't yet know it, customers want something better, and your desire to delight customers will drive you to invent on their behalf."

Beautifully, wonderfully dissatisfied—it's our job (and challenge) as product managers to understand this.

KEEPTRUCKIN, ELDS, AND HOURS OF SERVICE

For this customer analysis discussion, I want to use the example of KeepTruckin, a newer San Francisco based-company that helps transportation fleets in the U.S. and Canada stay compliant with regulations. KeepTruckin, backed by Google Ventures and other investors, dove into the trucking and transportation industry because they felt it was ripe for disruption.

In the U.S., federal rules prevent drivers in commercial fleets from driving more than eleven hours in one day, or working more than fourteen hours in one day, and working more than seventy hours during an eight-day period. Drivers also need to punctuate their days (or nights) with thirty-minute breaks. Rules in Canada vary slightly, but follow the same general theme as the U.S.

With a new U.S. Department of Transportation mandate in place, all vehicles subject to these federal rules need an electronic logging device (ELD) installed to track a driver's hours of service. The driver needs to record his or her status—driving, on-duty not driving, sleeper berth, off duty. The goal of these regulations is to prevent collisions caused by drowsy drivers.

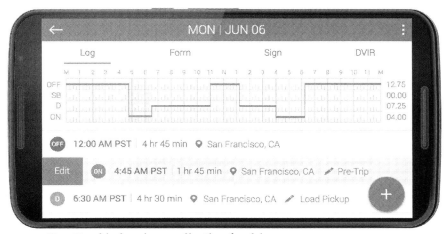

Figure 2.1: KeepTruckin logging application for drivers

KeepTruckin supplies trucking fleets with electronic logging devices—with software for drivers to accurately log their hours, and tools for back-office staff to effectively manage a compliance program across their full fleet, preventing violations.

You might think to be a product manager for a service that tracks drivers' hours of service would be dead boring—the kind of job that would induce the drowsiness the federal regulations are designed to prevent. The job of fleet compliance manager—the staff that is charged with ensuring that drivers comply with all hours-of-service regulations—might seem like the pinnacle of boredom.

Fortunately, neither of those things is true. Our job as a product manager means we get to go outside and talk to people, and if you meet with compliance managers at commercial fleets, you'll find they are passionate about their work.

They will tell you about a driver in Montana that refuses to take thirty-minute breaks, despite repeated warnings. You will hear how strongly they feel about keeping their drivers and their companies out of compliance trouble—avoiding the fines, audits, and penalties associated with fleets that manage hours of service poorly. And you will learn how important it is for them to get their drivers home safely at night—avoiding the catastrophic collisions caused by drowsy drivers. They will also give you an earful about your solution: what's working, what's not, and what they want changed.

In an area as seemingly dull as hours-of-service compliance management, customers are committed and passionate about what they do. Even if things are going well, they are, to use Jeff Bezos' words, beautifully, wonderfully dissatisfied. It's our job (and privilege) as product managers to understand the depths of this.

ETHNOGRAPHIC RESEARCH

We can, and should, learn about our customers in multiple ways. We can do research, we can share prototypes and gauge customer reaction, we can do market testing (like AB tests), and we can track how customers use our products.

This work can be qualitative—where we have deep conversations with a smaller set of customers (to speak mathematically, n = few). It can also be quantitative, for example, surveys with a larger set of customers and potential customers (n = many). It can also pull in big data (n = all).

One of the simplest and most direct ways of understanding customer needs for us product managers is ethnographic research. This technique came out of the field of anthropology, and despite the fancy name, it is reasonably straightforward. For us product managers, ethnographic research means interviews and observation of customers where they use our products (or our competitors' products).

To conduct this research, I'll suggest seven steps. We'll go through each of these in turn.

Ethnographic research: 7 steps	
Before the interview	1. Clarify your objectives
	2. Recruit people for interviews
	3. Develop a discussion guide
During the interview	4. Conduct the interview
After the interview	5. Capture your notes
	6. Tease out key themes
	7. Share with your team

Figure 2.2: Steps for ethnographic research

Clarify Your Objectives

Clarifying your objectives is a starting point for any serious market research. Even if it is just a short list, you should note the key goals of your research. Begin with your broad overarching objective, for example, to gain a deep, qualitative understanding of your customers' needs and motivations to help guide next-generation products. Follow with your specific objectives. For example, get early feedback on new product concepts (more about this on Day 6).

Recruit People for Interviews

You should focus on your target customer segment, and recruit people across the spectrum to ensure a diversity of views:

- Your customers
- Your competitors' customers
- Potential customers who aren't yet using your product (or competing products)

Your sales or client services teams can help you connect with your customers—and with people that went with competitors or have decided not to purchase.

If you are new to a market and don't yet have customers, you can hire a market research firm to recruit respondents for you. Sometimes this works well, although for many markets it makes more sense to reach out to potential customers directly.

Be creative here. The electronic logging device company, KeepTruckin, simply went to truck stops in California and started interviewing truck drivers (maybe in exchange for free hamburgers).

Develop a Discussion Guide

A best practice for ethnographic research is to write a discussion guide before interviewing. For anthropologists heading into the highlands of Papua New Guinea, this might be challenging. However, for us product managers, these discussion guides tend to follow a standard format.

I'll outline an approach in Figure 2.3 and describe these in the following section. You will need to adapt and modify this to match your product and your objectives.

Discussion guide outline	
Introduction and purpose	• Introduce yourself and your team • State the purpose of your research • Emphasize that you want honest and open feedback ("you won't hurt our feelings")
Customer background	• Find out more about the customer (job, responsibilities, day-to-day work, etc.) • Find out more about the company, if relevant (area of specialization, size of company, branch offices, customers, growth, etc.)
Customer needs	• Find out what is working well and not working well today • What would they like to see? How would this help them? • Probe to understand needs, priorities, and underlying motivations • Observe them as they use your product (or your competitor's product)
Product concepts	• Share draft concepts for future products and get their initial feedback
Thanks and next steps	• Restate the purpose of your research • Talk through any follow-ups (further testing, beta testing, etc.) • Thank them for the feedback

Figure 2.3: Discussion guide outline

Conduct the Interviews

You should meet your users as close to the line of action as possible. For example, if you are researching U.S. truck drivers, go to truck stops (as the staff at KeepTruckin did). If you are researching how small businesses use color laser printers and copiers, visit these customers at their offices—preferably at their desks, at the printer, at the copier, and preferably not sequestered inside a conference room. If you are a product manager for DNA testing services at Ancestry, talk to customers at the very moment they get their results back.

Remember that we are observing as much as we are listening, and you need context for this—you won't be able to observe much if you invite customers into your office, or peek at them from behind a focus group window.

You'll want to follow your discussion guide, but be flexible rather than scripted. Dive in when you hear items you didn't expect—follow your curiosity. Every interview is different because every customer is different. If you have fifteen to twenty in-depth interviews with customers, you won't need to cover every item in your discussion guide during every interview.

Let's step through the different parts of the interview.

Introduction and Purpose

Start by introducing yourself (or your team) and stating your purpose. For us product managers, the purpose is usually easy—we want to know more about our customers and their needs to help design better products in the future. Customers, especially for business-to-business products, are usually very willing to help—they want to give their perspective, they feel happy to be asked, and they share our goal of making our products a better match for their needs.

You should mention that you will be talking to multiple customers, and then returning to your extended team to map out future direction based on the feedback. You will want to tactfully set the tone that not every item they request is going to get done—you will be consolidating their input with all other input and making the best choices for the product.

You should ask for open and honest feedback. Stress that the goal is to develop products that better match your customers' needs, and to do this you need to hear the good, the bad, and the ugly. Tell the customer that they can't hurt your feelings, and make sure you mirror this attitude during the interview—always being receptive, curious, non-judgmental, and never defensive.

Customer Background

Next, find out more about your customer and, if relevant, their company. We'll dive into customer needs surrounding your product in the next part of the interview, but in this section, try to understand your customers' context and what they are trying to do.

If you were a product manager for KeepTruckin and interviewing compliance managers at trucking fleets, you'd want to know the size of their fleet, who their customers are, what types of transportation services they offer, how many remote sites they have, etc. You would also ask about the role of the person you are interviewing, and how they fit within the broader organization.

Customer Needs

Now that you have the basic context, you can start to tease out what the customer is trying to do: what are the jobs to be done, what are the pains they are trying to avoid, and what are the gains they are seeking.

One tool to initiate the discussion is to ask what is working well today, and what is not working well. Better yet, have customers show you. Have them step through a "day in the life" of how they use your product. This is especially helpful for software products, but is also relevant for hardware.

As part of your interview, you'll want to ask a series of "whys" (and "whats" and "hows") to uncover underlying motivations. Why is this important to you? How does it help you? Why do you care about this? What is your goal?

Sometimes (oftentimes) our customers will ask for very specific enhancements ("I want a report that lists all drivers who used their trucks yesterday for personal conveyance of more than 10 miles/16 km"). It is good to note these, but don't get distracted. Our learning goal is to delve into the context and underlying motivations. Remember we are trying to get to the articulated and unarticulated needs of our customers. The more we can get to the underlying motivations—rather than surface level requests—the better we will be at developing breakthrough products.

Product Concepts

These types of interviews are good opportunities to get feedback on new product concepts. You can share simple mockups to get feedback. Would this help you? How? What would you like changed to better meet your needs? Remember that even if these new product concepts are your pride and joy, you need to appear neutral, open, and receptive to less-than-enthusiastic responses. We'll talk more about how to do this in the Day 6: Discovery and Delivery section.

Thanks and Next Steps

Check with your customer if there is anything important that you haven't asked. Thank them for their time, and reiterate that their feedback will be used to guide next-generation product development to better meet their needs. You may want to ask about potential follow-ups—for example, you can ask if they would like to be a beta site in the future.

Capture Your Notes

Consolidate and organize your notes quickly after your interview. This type of research is all about detail and anecdotes, and if you wait a day or two, your memory won't be as fresh (at least mine isn't), and you'll miss insights.

Make sure to capture your immediate impressions and anything that surprised you. If you are conducting research with your colleagues, go to a coffee shop and debrief.

Tease out Key Themes

When you complete a critical mass of interviews (typically ten to fifteen interviews), review all your notes, and tease out key themes. Share these themes with the colleagues who joined you on the research and add their insight and depth. Don't rush this step; it takes thinking, digestion, sifting, prodding, and discussion. Document your findings in a presentation or report.

Share with Your Team

Share your findings broadly with your team. Use the insights to guide your strategic work as a product manager—developing breakthrough products, optimizing pricing, and finding growth.

Tips for Success

Ethnographic research is central to what we do as product managers. We strive for a deep understanding of the articulated and unarticulated needs of our customers, and ethnographic research is one of our best tools.

Getting good at these types of interviews takes practice. The best product managers have done hundreds of them.

I'll pass along a few tips—some you'll find in the anthropology textbooks, and some you won't.

Listen and Observe Far More Than You Talk

Listening and observing (versus talking) should be obvious, but product managers often make mistakes here. If you record one of your interviews, you shouldn't hear your voice more than 20% of the time. The focus should be on the customer, and their thoughts, ideas, and perspective.

Start Broad, Then Go Narrow

We want to hear what truly matters to our customers—and to do this, we need to give them space to tell us. Start with broad, open-ended questions. Our natural instincts as product managers are to delve into very specific items, but probing for details up front can bias later answers.

Act like an Outsider

As a product manager, you are an expert in your area—a consummate insider. Some market research professionals argue that product managers shouldn't be doing their own research, precisely because of this issue and the bias that it brings. To correct for this, you should take on the persona of an outsider, and put your expertise aside. If customers ask questions during the interview, politely defer these to the end of the discussion. Keep the focus on the customer's perspective during the interview.

Do This Research Together with Your Colleagues

Go with your lead engineer, go with your user experience (UX) designer. Research is much more effective firsthand, and your colleagues will have insight you might miss.

Be Careful of Sales Reps

We love sales representatives, but they can work at cross-purposes during ethnographic research. I was with a customer recently that mischaracterized our product and its features. A sales representative's natural instincts are to correct this, but if you correct customers during interviews, they will be less open with you afterward, fearing they'll make another mistake. Remember the point of these interviews is to thoroughly understand our customers' perspectives, and not to push our views. Two options for sales reps and ethnographic research are: to keep them out of the room, or ask them to hold their questions and comments until the end.

I hope you enjoy ethnographic research. For me, it is one of the best parts of product management—completely energizing and engaging.

ANALYZING CUSTOMER NEEDS

After your first pulse of ethnographic research, you will come back to your cubicle with a mound of anecdotes and a mess of user needs. To make use of all this research, you'll want to analyze customer needs in more depth.

I'm going to suggest two methods for analyzing customer needs: the Kano model and benefit trees. Let's start with the Kano model.

KANO MODEL

Your customers (or potential customers) are trying to solve an issue or realize an opportunity. They are trying to satisfy their needs.

However, not all needs are equal. Customers have different priorities and meanings attached to these needs, and as a product manager, you need to understand this.

The Kano model can help with this process. This approach was developed by the Japanese professor, Noriaki Kano, in the 1980s to help categorize and prioritize customer needs, to guide new product development and to enhance customer satisfaction. It's a very useful tool.

Let's start with the model's axes. On the x-axis, we can plot how well a need was met—poorly (or not met at all) or met very well. On the y-axis, we can chart how we feel about this—disgusted to delighted. Using this simple graph, we can start separating and analyzing customer needs. See Figure 2.4.

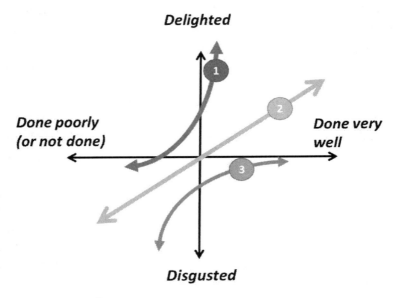

Delighted

**Done poorly
(or not done)**

**Done very
well**

Disgusted

1 **Attractive needs (delighters)**
Unspoken, not expected
- Need 1
- Need 2
- Need 3

2 **Performance needs**
Stated, more is better
- Need 1
- Need 2
- Need 3

3 **Basic needs**
"Must be" requirements
- Need 1
- Need 2
- Need 3

Figure 2.4: Kano model

To understand the model, let's use a simple example of flying from San Diego (where my wife and I live) to Tokyo (where our son and daughter live). When we travel, we sometimes check luggage—and our need is to not only get ourselves to Japan, but also get our bags there. If our luggage shows up on the carousel in Tokyo, we pick it up and leave. We aren't thrilled that our luggage made it, we don't jump for joy or give each other high-fives, we just expected this. However, if our luggage didn't show up, my wife and I would not be happy—or, to use the model's language, we'd be disgusted. Luggage is an example of a basic need. Basic needs are "must-be" requirements for any product or service.

We also want the flight to be comfortable, convenient, and affordable. These are all performance needs—and companies compete to best satisfy these needs. On the flight from San Diego to Tokyo, Japan Airlines has direct flights, pleasant service, a good movie selection, and my favorite Yebisu beer. From a customer standpoint, typically more is better with performance needs (except for price).

If my wife and I are very lucky, we might get upgraded to business class. If this doesn't happen, I don't feel negative about it—I wasn't expecting it in the first place. However, if it does, I'm delighted. Complimentary upgrades are a good example of an attractive need.

After ethnographic research with your target customers, you'll come back with a host of notes, especially about all their various needs. Using the Kano model is an easy way to separate these needs into three categories and draw additional insight.

We'll talk about new product development later, but this model also helps guide feature and functionality choices. For any product or service, you must meet the basic needs or customers won't consider you. There is no real choice here. For the performance needs, chose the right set at the right level to ensure an attractive, competitive product. And pick one or two attractive needs for competitive differentiation and customer delight.

When you use this model, give a mental "thanks" to Professor Kano. He did good work.

BENEFIT TREES

In our ethnographic research, we asked a number of "whys." Why is this important? Why is this motivating? If we do this research correctly, we end up with a hierarchy of customer needs and can begin to map the relationships of these needs (and corresponding product benefits).

Benefit trees are a way to map this hierarchy, and this visualization can help guide both our product development choices as well as our outbound product messaging.

Let's go back to our KeepTruckin example and put yourself into the well-worn shoes of their product manager. Remember that this company provides in-vehicle, electronic logging devices for truckers to record their driving and non-driving hours. The company also supplies a back-office web service that helps fleet compliance managers monitor all their drivers.

From ethnographic research with truck drivers and compliance managers at major U.S. transportation fleets, you would have heard a laundry list of needs and, using KeepTruckin's device and services—a laundry list of benefits. Let's list them:

- Ease of use for new drivers
- Decrease hours-of-service log errors
- Spend less time correcting non-compliant logs
- Avoid fines
- Reduce drowsy driving
- Reduce collisions
- Avoid costly lawsuits
- Reduce my fleet operating costs
- Save lives

You might look at this list and be understandably puzzled on next steps. The benefits themselves span from the ground level (easy to use for new drivers) to the critical (save lives). Some are focused on money (avoid fines) while others are focused on safety (reduce drowsy driving). Also, different people within a fleet will value these benefits differently—for example, a truck driver might put a high priority on "ease of use" while a compliance manager might focus on "spend less time correcting non-compliant logs."

Benefit trees can help provide structure. Look at Figure 2.5, which uses the same list of benefits as above.

Figure 2.5: Benefit tree

Starting at the bottom, the KeepTruckin log devices are easy to use for new drivers. Because of this, they make fewer errors and compliance managers spend less time correcting them. Fewer errors also mean fewer government fines, and the benefits "less time correcting logs" and "avoid fines" help reduce a fleet's operating costs.

There is also a safety component to these benefits. Decreased log errors mean drivers are less likely to drive when they shouldn't be—reducing drowsy driving. This leads to fewer collisions, which helps avoid major lawsuits and ultimately reduces a fleet's operating costs. More importantly, fewer collisions mean saved lives.

These trees can clarify an unruly set of customer benefits, and they can also guide communication to specific target audiences. In the KeepTruckin example, if the company was to reach out to truckers, they would probably want to emphasize how easy their electronic logging device is to use, and how truckers make fewer log errors with their device. If they were communicating with compliance managers, "less time correcting logs" and "avoid fines" would probably be the messages that best resonate. CEOs might be concerned about the full gamut, but may be especially focused on reducing their fleet operating costs. Safety managers will be most interested in reducing drowsy driving, reducing collisions and saving lives. See Figure 2.6.

Figure 2.6: Benefit tree with communication targets

You'll have to try this with your product—see if you can map out a benefit tree. These trees can provide clarity to the mess of customer needs and benefits that we discover during our ethnographic research. They can help guide our new product development as well as our customer communication.

DAY 2 FINAL WORDS

Becoming a more strategic product manager starts with a deep, intuitive understanding of our customers. To create market-leading, breakthrough products—to create a remarkable customer journey—we need to listen and observe with curiosity, openness, and passion. Our customers are "beautifully, wonderfully dissatisfied" in the words of Jeff Bezos. As product managers, this is where we dive in.

DAY 2 ON ONE PAGE

1. A **deep, intuitive understanding of our customers** is a foundational element of product management. Jeff Bezos writes that "customers are always beautifully, wonderfully dissatisfied." It's our job as product managers to understand this.

2. **Ethnographic research** is one of our best and simplest tools to understand customer needs and motivations. For us product managers, this means interviewing and observing customers as closely as possible to the line of action—where and when they are using our products.

3. During ethnographic research, we need to take on the role of a **curious, open, receptive outsider**, not the industry insider we are on most days. We need to actively listen to customer perspectives, starting with broad, open-ended questions, and then narrowing later.

4. Not all customer needs are equal, and customers attach different meanings and priorities to these. The **Kano model** is a useful tool to analyze customer needs—separating them into basic, performance, and attractive needs.

5. **Benefit trees** can help us map customer needs (and corresponding product benefits) into an intelligible hierarchy. We can use these trees to steer product development as well as customer communication.

DAY 3: COMPETITIVE ANALYSIS

Direct and Disruptive

Developing a long-term competitive advantage is one of the pillars of our work as product managers. Competitive advantage is not an ethereal or theoretical concept, but is something very concrete—we need to be better than all competing alternatives at meeting our customers' needs.

To develop this competitive advantage—to make it a systematic part of our work as product managers—we need to monitor and analyze our competitors. Every product manager on the planet knows this, it's not some hidden surprise. Unfortunately, most of us, buried in day-to-day tactical requests, underinvest in competitive analysis.

WHY ANALYZE COMPETITORS?

Why should we analyze competitors? A few different reasons:

Anticipate market shifts. Our markets are not static—they drift, meander, and evolve. Living inside a single company, we can become blind to this, seeing the market with our own biased eyes. Closely monitoring competitors can help us identify changes in the market that we might have otherwise missed.

Spot the emergence of new competitors. Established, market-leading companies often get surprised by the success of unanticipated competitors, who have new features, lower pricing, or a slightly different target customer. Closely watching the competitive landscape can get ahead of these surprises.

Craft counter-attack strategies. Good competitive analysis can guide the best ways for us to punch back at our competitors, and steal their market share.

Optimize pricing. We'll talk about pricing on Day 7, but knowing the prices of your top competitors is critical to optimizing your pricing, and meeting your profitability and growth goals.

Improve your product or service. As product managers, we do our research, work with our engineering teams, and strive to develop products that delight our customers. But we don't always get it right and competing companies may scoop us on a particular feature or product. Monitoring and analyzing our competitors can give us early visibility on these good ideas, and (assuming they aren't patent protected) we can adapt and incorporate these ideas into our product. Think of this as a form of crowdsourcing.

IDENTIFYING AND PRIORITIZING COMPETITORS

Answering the question "who are your competitors?" can be deceptively difficult. At one level, the answer is simple—it might be a company you lost a deal to yesterday. However, there are also groups of competitors that offer something slightly different than you, and others are offering entirely new ways of meeting the needs of the same customer.

Let's think about competitors in three different categories: direct, category, and disruptive.

Direct Competition

These competitors are the easiest to identify because you meet them every day in the market. They offer very similar products and services, targeted at the same customer needs.

I worked for many years at HP and was a product manager for color laser printers. At HP we were in a market-leading position worldwide, but had a full set of direct competitors—like Samsung, Brother, and Xerox— who were offering very similar color laser printers.

Category Competition

For many products, there is a set of category competitors, who are meeting the same basic customer needs with a slightly different product approach. Inkjet printers are a category competitor for HP's color laser printers.

Substitutes, Market Evolution, and Disruptive Technology

With this category of competitors, customers meet their needs in fundamentally new or different ways.

When I was working at HP, we worried about direct color laser printer competitors, and competing inkjet printers, but the real competitive threat was from disruptive technology.

Paper—the printed page—offers portable, easy-to-use and easy-to-share access to information. But smartphones, tablets, and laptops offer this same portable information access (in fact, better access in many respects).

I remember one interview with a customer where I asked about printing from a mobile device. I got a blank look, and then an answer something along the line of "isn't the point of mobile technology that we don't need to print?" We saw this in our market sizing reports—the rise of mobile technology caused a corresponding drop in pages going to office printers.

We'll take a deeper look at disruptive technology later in this section.

WHAT TO ANALYZE

For our direct competitors, I'll list eight areas we should dive into.

Market Share and Trends

You should include the market share for your product and your main competitors, and whether this is trending up or down. If you think about all the customers who purchased a category of products during a given time, what percentage purchased from you? What percentage from competitor A? What percentage from competitor B?

When I've consulted with various product management teams, the eyes of product managers sometimes grow wide when I ask this. For some markets, we have industry analysts that compile market share statistics, but for most markets, this third-party information is non-existent.

My recommendation, if you don't have easily accessible market share data, is to estimate this. You will know your sales, and you will have an idea of the total market size—and from these two numbers, you can estimate your market share. You will also have a sense of your competitors, and whether they have higher or lower share than you.

Having a rough estimate of market share will give you a better picture of the market than having no estimate. You can make this more accurate over time as you gain new information.

Strategy and Investments

Your competitors are not standing still, they are evolving and improving their products. They have a direction, and you want to know where they are headed. You'll want to know their major investments, what types of people they are hiring, what hints they are giving in their press releases or public comments, and what they are saying to their key clients.

This work takes triangulation from multiple sources—published reports, YouTube videos, industry analysts, patent filings, job postings, and friendly customers who may talk to you after your competitor shows up at their door.

We'll talk about the San Francisco-based company, Nauto, in our Day 4 strategy discussion, but they serve as a good example here as well. A glance at Nauto's job openings provides a strong indicator of their future direction, both in terms of technology as well as geography. Recent jobs included openings for a "VP of computer vision and deep learning," and a second for a "Business development manager, fleets in Japan."

Target Markets

Which key market segments or customers are your competitors targeting? Is their target different than yours? Knowing their primary and secondary targets can help you understand your competitors' market actions and next steps.

Strengths and Weaknesses

It is easy to see our competitors as the corporate incarnation of Darth Vader, but try to spell out your competitors' strengths and weaknesses with clear eyes, as a third-party analyst would. We'll get to competitive selling-against tools later, but note here that your sales representatives hate getting surprised in front of customers—they want to be forewarned of both the pluses and minuses of your competitors' offerings.

One of the best ways to understand the strengths and weaknesses of competing products is to become a user yourself. Trying your competitors' offering is easier with business-to-consumer products (B2C), and more difficult with business-to-business products (B2B). Many B2B products are sold directly to customers, and your competitors may block a sale to you. If you can get your hands on competing products (or experience competing services), try to step through the products as a normal user would, and identify what your competitors have done well, and the areas they have done less well.

Additional sources of competitive strengths and weaknesses are websites, blogs, customer support pages, and social media channels where competing products are discussed. These are great sources of unfiltered user comments.

Technology Position

If you are in a market dominated by technology, what is the technology position of your competitors? Are they protected by a wall of patents? Do they have a lead on you in a particular area, or are they lagging in key areas?

Pricing

How are your competitors pricing, and what are their prices? Are their pricing models like yours, or are they pricing differently? For example, are their models using monthly subscription pricing versus one-time payments?

Pricing analysis is easier in the business-to-consumer space, where prices are usually up front and published. In the B2B space, competitive pricing can be trickier to discern. B2B pricing is often hidden and negotiated on a client-by-client basis.

Even in B2B situations, however, you can usually get a solid sense of your competitors' pricing. Your sales representatives may learn competitive pricing in enterprise deals where you are competing head-to-head. Also, transparency rules may mean that bids for government contracts are open and accessible.

Channel Strategy

How are your competitors reaching their customers? Are they selling direct online or direct via their own sales representatives, or are they selling through third-party channel partners (like distributors or value-added resellers)?

Reaction Pattern

With this analysis, our goal is to anticipate and predict the market moves of our competitors. One method for doing this is to look at their historical reaction patterns. For example, when you launched a major new feature or product in the past, how did your competitor respond? Did they immediately copy this feature with press releases and fanfare to the market? Did they quietly incorporate your best ideas into their product over time? Or did they ignore you?

As another example, when you launched a market promotion (e.g., a bundled offering at a lower price during a key buying season) did your competitors immediately match this?

Cataloging the past reaction patterns of your competitors can help you predict their actions in response to your next move.

DOCUMENTING YOUR ANALYSIS

A side-by-side table (Figure 3.1) can help you document and share your analysis. A stacked-area chart (Figure 3.2) can help you visualize and communicate market size and share dynamics. See example charts below.

This analysis is not rocket science—in fact, it is not that difficult to do. It is, however, part of being a disciplined and strategic product manager. If you can understand your competitors and anticipate their next moves, you can go a long way toward crafting long-term competitive advantages for your product.

Competition comparison table			
	Your company	**Competitor A**	**Competitor B**
Market share & trends	X%	Y%	Z%
Strategy & investments			
Target markets	*Detail*	*Detail*	*Detail*
Strengths	*your*	*your*	*your*
Weaknesses	*company*	*competitors*	*competitors*
Technology position	*in*	*in*	*in*
Pricing	*this*	*these*	*these*
Channel strategy	*column*	*columns*	*columns*
Reaction pattern			

Figure 3.1: Competition comparison table

MARKET SIZE AND SHARE
in million euros

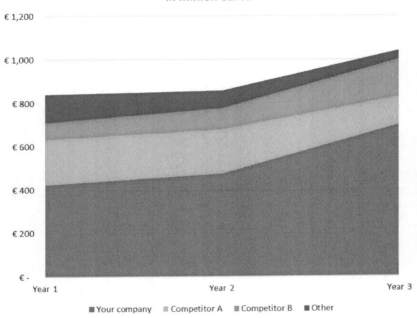

Figure 3.2: Market size and share sample chart

COMPETITIVE POSITIONING

An insightful tool for us product managers is a competitive positioning matrix. I'll describe this at a high level, then illustrate this with an example.

Let's start with a simple matrix, with the two axes representing areas of critical competition. For example, the x-axis and y-axis might represent speed, performance, quality, price, ease of use, customer support, etc.,—all on a low-high scale.

The choice for each axis takes critical thinking—you'll need to determine areas of competition that are insightful and meaningful. Each of your axes should be something on which customers place a high value.

Next, plot yourself and your competitors. Remember to do this with objective eyes, accurately representing yourself and your competitors: as product managers we have a natural affection for our products, but keep this bias out of the picture.

Finally, use the competitive analysis we described above, and add some arrows. Which direction are you moving? Where are your competitors headed? See Figure 3.3.

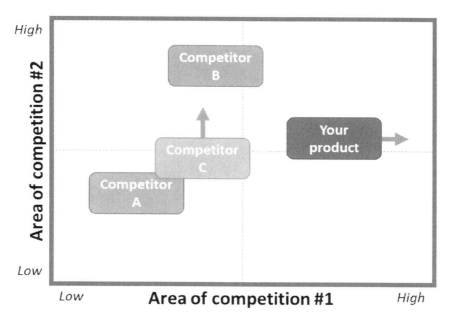

Figure 3.3: Competitive positioning matrix

Let's go back to KeepTruckin, the company that offers electronic logging solutions for truck drivers and trucking companies. Because of all the good ethnographic research KeepTruckin did with drivers, and because they are a newer Silicon Valley/Bay Area company, the solution they designed is very easy for drivers to use. If you were a product manager at KeepTruckin, you would know this is an area of critical importance when fleet managers decide on an electronic logging device. Let's put "driver friendliness/ease of use" on the x-axis.

Another area of tough competition is the completeness of the electronic logging device solution. For example, does it include fleet tracking, state-by-state tax reporting, engine diagnostics, geofencing, messaging? Let's make the y-axis "service offering" to represent the comprehensiveness of the solution.

KeepTruckin has two very entrenched, long-established competitors in this space—Omnitracs and PeopleNet. There are also many smaller competitors, with varying degrees of market success.

Because Omnitracs and PeopleNet have been in the market for many years, both companies have built a full suite of services for trucking firms. They both score very high on the y-axis (service offering). On the other hand, KeepTruckin—with its newer Silicon Valley-influenced user interface—is more driver friendly.

As a final step, add a future direction. Do we think Omnitracs and PeopleNet will refresh their user interface and move to the right, or will they focus on continuing to build on their very full suite of extended applications and move up our chart? And if you were the product manager for KeepTruckin, you and your team would have strategic choices to make: do you focus your development efforts on completing your service offering to match Omnitracs or PeopleNet, or do you extend your driver-friendliness advantage?

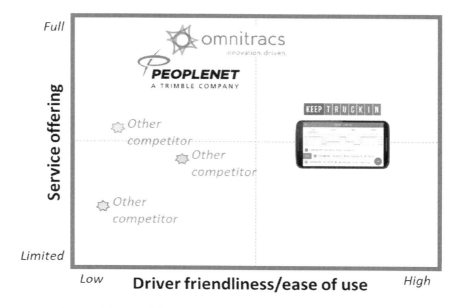

Figure 3.4: Competitive positioning matrix example for the electronic logging device market

This competitive positioning matrix is a good way to synthesize your more detailed, competitive analysis. Your executives will readily understand this chart, and recognize its importance for customer communication, market positioning, and long-term strategy.

COMPETITIVE SELLING–AGAINST TOOLS

Competitive selling-against tools are a very common request from sales teams and can make them more confident in the face of competition, and more successful. You can use your competitive analysis to craft impactful selling-against tools for your biggest competitors.

See Figure 3.5 for a basic format you can use for competitive selling-against tools. A few notes:

- You will likely need versions of this tool for each of your major competitors.
- The top left graphic is the competitive matrix we discussed earlier.
- The top right box provides a basic description of the competitor's product.
- In the middle, highlight three or four compelling advantages that you have versus a competing product. These advantages will be a summary of what your sales reps can say in competitive head-to-head deals.
- In the lower left box, spell out what competitors will claim. Customers may reiterate these to your sales reps—challenging them—and you want your sales teams prepared with credible answers.
- In the lower right box, compare your product versus a competing product, highlighting the strengths and weaknesses of different benefits and supporting features.

Note that you may need to get your legal team's "OK" on these, even if the tools are only used internally by your company's own sales representatives.

Selling-against tools, when done well, help sales reps counter competitive pressure, and help them win deals. Do these right, and you'll be the sales team's favorite product manager.

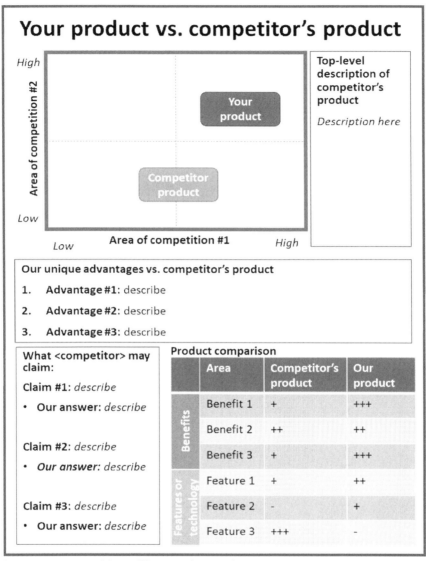

Figure 3.5: Competitive selling-against tool

DISRUPTIVE TECHNOLOGY

Beyond direct and category competition, we need to be alert to disruptive technologies. Disruptive technologies are innovations in product, service, or business models that fundamentally alter market demand. Long-established companies can lose their market position, even companies that have historically had excellent management and high profits.

Even the best companies face risks with disruptive technologies, and internal dynamics can make companies more susceptible: a culture of not facing hard issues, lack of imagination, resistance to change, high customer demands, and high profitability.

The last two factors need explanation. High customer demands divert a management team's attention to the immediate and less consequential, and away from the long-term and substantial. Inside a company, high customer demands also create the illusion of responsibly responding to the market. Unfortunately, a focus on the day-to-day waves misses the upcoming tsunami.

High profitability is an interesting one since on the surface you would think a nice cash flow would give companies the capability to become next-generation leaders in disruptive technology. In reality, high profits can make a company protective and conservative, with no new business opportunities looking as attractive as the current business.

Let's look at two examples of disruptive technologies, one that has already happened (digital photography) and one that is coming (autonomous vehicles).

Kodak

Kodak is Exhibit A for a disruptive technology discussion. Throughout most of the twentieth century, Kodak was a remarkably innovative and successful company. Based in upstate New York, the company invented roll film, and in the mid-1970s, sold 90% of the photographic film and 85% of the cameras in the U.S. In 1986, the company employed 145,000 people. Today, after filing for chapter 11 bankruptcy protection, the company employs about 6,000 people.

The market for photographic film collapsed over the past twenty years, replaced by a set of disruptive technologies—digital photography, digital cameras (embedded in phones), and online sharing. Kodak's downfall wasn't inevitable, however. Between 1970 and 2000, it was arguably the best-positioned company in the world to lead digital photography.

In 1975, an engineer at Kodak, Steve Sasson, created a toaster-sized instrument that could digitally save an image. This instrument was the world's first digital camera. Sasson demonstrated the technology to Kodak management, but was met with blank faces. At the time, these managers could not grasp the potential.

Later, when Kodak's managers fully understood the impact of digital photography, they put their development and release of digital cameras in slow gear, in hopes of protecting their very profitable film business.

Carly Fiorina, in a 2007 interview, summarized Kodak's situation well: "Kodak sat on a mountain of cash and profitability in their traditional photography business, and I believe their thinking was digital photography will eat into my traditional profitable business. I don't want that to happen. What I think Kodak miscalculated about was they weren't in charge of whether that would happen. Consumers were in charge ... suddenly consumers had a new way of taking pictures that gave them more control, more freedom, more flexibility, and more choice. The consumer became in charge of how fast Kodak's traditional business would be eaten away. And Kodak, unfortunately, didn't see that in time."

Kodak is a good historical caution for us product managers. Failure to respond to disruptive technology can be endemic throughout the organization, but as product managers, we play a key role in preventing this. We can't limit our competitive analysis to direct competitors, but need an eyes-wide-open view of disruptive technologies—both the threats and the opportunities.

Autonomous Vehicles

Disruptive technologies haven't stopped with digital photography, and we (as product managers) and we (as humans) are in for a doozie over the next ten to twenty years. With the advent of autonomous vehicles, we are moving from a world where vehicles are driven by humans, to one where vehicles drive themselves; from a world of petroleum-powered internal combustion engines to one far more electric; from private car ownership to mobility-as-a-service (MaaS).

We will go from our transportation life today, where we have a high number of vehicles, mostly parked, to an environment with a lower number of vehicles, mostly used. Our vehicles will move from being independent and discrete (I don't think my Toyota Prius connects to anything, other than radio stations) to vehicles that connect to other vehicles, and connect to our transportation infrastructure. And there is one big transition that can't come soon enough—we will move from a world where traffic fatalities are horribly common to a world that is far safer to drive in.

Many of us product managers will face autonomous vehicles as a disruptive technology for our businesses. And autonomous vehicles will be a disruptive technology in the fullest sense of the word—both in the "our business is going down the tubes" sense as well as the "we have unbelievable new opportunities" sense.

It's hard to list all the industries that will be impacted, but let's look at a partial list:

- Vehicle manufacture and sales
- Vehicle insurance
- Parking lots
- Driver safety and compliance
- Trucking and distribution
- Last-mile package delivery
- Fueling stations
- Urban planning
- Public transportation
- Road construction
- And many more

Airports in the U.S. are already actively considering the impact of autonomous vehicles when they evaluate new parking structures. Parking structures have a thirty-year investment horizon, and it is unclear if airports will need extensive parking in thirty years. If you are a product manager for parking lots (are there parking lot product managers?) you are already dealing with autonomous vehicles as a disruptive technology.

The bottom line is that a large chunk of us product managers are facing—or will very soon face—autonomous vehicles as a disruptive technology. If you are in an affected industry, make sure to incorporate this into your competitive analysis, and consider both the threats and opportunities in your product strategy work.

COMPETITIVE MONITORING

As product managers, we should have an ongoing process of competitive monitoring and analysis. I'll suggest three different time scales:

- *Continuous:* This is weekly, ongoing monitoring of your direct competitors to spot when they launch a new feature or product, when they start a new promotion, or when their CEO says something intriguing about their future strategy. Try to automate this if you can, for example with Google alerts.
- *Periodic:* Most of this Day 3 discussion has been around deep-dive competitive analysis—looking at your direct and category competitors, as well as disruptive technology. You should do this deep analysis once every three months, or at least once every six months.
- *Project-based:* At times, your competitors will surprise you with a new, innovative, market-changing product, and you'll want to dive in with a full analysis. Project-based analysis happens on an as-needed basis.

DAY 3 FINAL WORDS

To become a more strategic product manager, we need to generate long-term, competitive advantage for our products. Competitive advantage requires work across the product management spectrum—encompassing a deep understanding of our customers, strategy development, and side-by-side work with our development teams to create products that delight customers.

Underpinning all of this is a solid analysis of our competitors and their direction, as well as an eyes-open view of disruptive technologies.

My advice is to set aside time—on a quarterly or half-yearly basis—to thoroughly understand your competitors and their future direction, as well the threats and opportunities of disruptive technologies.

DAY 3 ON ONE PAGE

1. A key purpose of product management is to generate a **long-term, competitive advantage** for our products, and underpinning this is a thorough understanding of our competitors. Most of us product managers, however, underinvest in competitive analysis.

2. We should **analyze competitors** for many reasons: to anticipate market shifts, to spot the emergence of new competitors, to craft counter-attack strategies, to optimize pricing, and to improve our products and services.

3. We can think of our competitors in three categories: **direct** competitors, **category** competitors, and **disruptive** technologies.

4. When we **analyze direct competitors**, we should look at market share, strategy, target markets, strengths, weaknesses, technology position, pricing, channel strategy, and reaction pattern.

5. Mapping ourselves versus our competitors in a **competitive positioning matrix**—with key areas of competition on the x- and y-axis—can lead to new insights, and offers a condensed way of communicating competitive strategy with our executives.

6. Taking a sober, eyes-wide-open view of **disruptive technologies**—both the opportunities and threats—is critical to keep our products (and businesses) healthy, vibrant, and competitive in the long-term.

DAY 4: STRATEGY

Going Big

Breakthrough products, customers that give us hugs, competitors that fade into irrelevance. We have ambitions for our products, we want to go big. Some product managers will stumble into success, but for most of us—with levels of luck trending toward the mean—going big takes strategy.

Strategy is critical, but—oddly, crazily—few of us product managers spend enough time here. We limp along with an implicit strategy or follow the semi-coherent path inherited from the prior product manager.

Product strategy is an integrated concept for how we will meet our objectives. It guides all our work, including roadmaps, product development priorities, and where to find growth. Product strategy nests within, and complements, a broader company strategy. As product managers, we lead this.

If you want to become a more strategic product manager—if you want to have more impact on your organization and your customers—you'll need to develop a product strategy, evolving and enhancing it over time. In our Day 4 discussion, we'll talk about how to do this.

STEPS FOR CREATING A PRODUCT STRATEGY

There are seven basic steps for creating a product strategy. I'll list them here, and detail them below.

1. Form a cross-functional team
2. Review your corporate strategy
3. Examine your market intelligence
4. Craft your vision and objectives
5. Analyze, think, and discuss
6. Share and enhance
7. Use and iterate

Form a Cross-Functional Team

Strategy work takes discussion, prodding, probing, dissecting, and critical thinking—it's best done in a group. The first step is to pull together a team—which might be you, a finance team representative, an engineering lead, a client services or sales team lead, and potentially a corporate strategist (if you have one in your company).

If you can, get an executive sponsor and a charter to do this work. Approach an executive, explain the importance of reworking and clarifying your product strategy, and ask that she act as (or recommend) an executive sponsor. A perfect executive response to this kind of request is something like, "Great idea. Can you come to our senior leadership meeting next month and present your strategy?"

If you are the product manager for a component of a larger product, you may want to join forces with your fellow product managers and develop a strategy at a product level, or even a product group level. The goal is to develop strategies with impact and relevance, and picking the right level is an important part of this.

Review Your Corporate Strategy

The product strategy you create should be well aligned with your corporate strategy. If you end up with a product strategy that is tangential or peripheral to your company's core focus, this may be a new growth opportunity, or it may be a strategy that has no support from the business.

As a starting point, you and your team should review the latest company vision, objectives, and strategy. For many companies, this is hazy, but do what you can.

Examine Your Market Intelligence

A foundation for good strategy work is solid market intelligence. You should relook—and potentially augment—your market segmentation and size analysis. In our Day 2 discussion, we stressed the need for a deep understanding of customer needs, and this is essential for an excellent strategy. Competitive analysis, of both direct competitors and disruptive technologies, helps guide our strategy development.

Depending on your product area, you may want to conduct a technology assessment. What is the state of the technology, who is driving it, and where is it headed? A regulatory analysis might also be needed. Is the regulatory landscape changing? Remember that we are looking for trends, looming threats, and emerging opportunities.

Craft Your Vision and Objectives

Your product vision states how the world will be a better place if you succeed, and it should be ambitious and compelling. Your objectives should be specific, with measurable goals to chart progress toward your vision. Vision and objectives are a big area of strategy work, and we'll speak more on this later.

Analyze, Think, and Discuss

Analyzing, thinking, and discussing—this is the hard work of strategy and it helps to have a framework. We will use Donald Hambrick and James Fredrickson's strategy diamond approach. In a later section, we will dive into this.

During this step, it helps to develop two to three alternative strategies—comparing against each other and gauging their relative merit.

Share and Enhance

When you have strategic alternatives and a recommended direction, articulate this in a crisp, clear presentation, and share with your executives. Your leadership team will have advice and insight, which you will want to incorporate into the strategy you select.

I've included a basic outline of a product strategy presentation in Figure 4.1. See what you think. You'll need to modify and adapt this to your product and company.

Draft outline Product strategy presentation	
Introduction and purpose	• Purpose of the presentation • Top level recommendation
Market background	• Market size • Customer needs • Competitive situation • Technology and regulatory trends
Proposed direction	• Product vision and objectives • Emerging opportunities • Strategic alternatives and proposed direction • Customer value proposition and competitive advantage
Actions and timeline	• Product roadmap • Development path
Financial projections	• Investments needed • Revenue and profit expected
The "ask"	• Summarize investments required and other help needed

Figure 4.1: Product strategy presentation outline

Use and Iterate

Use your strategy to drive your future product roadmap, guide new product development, and steer your growth plans.

Your product vision should be reasonably steady over time—it is meant to point a long-term path. Your strategy shouldn't change dramatically every three months, but you will need to revise and evolve your strategy based on market experience, customer feedback, and competitive response.

These are the seven steps, but two of them— "product vision and objectives" and "analyze, think and discuss" —need more clarity. Let's go into that now.

PRODUCT VISION AND OBJECTIVES

A product vision (step 4 above) articulates how the world will be a better place if you succeed. It should be ambitious, compelling, motivating, and inspiring. It speaks to the fundamental meaning and value of our products.

Let's look at good examples of a product vision.

Wikimedia Foundation

In its vision statement, the foundation that supports Wikipedia and related sites ask us to:

> *Imagine a world in which every single human being can freely share in the sum of all knowledge. That's our commitment.*

This vision is ambitious, compelling, and motivating. It makes me want to be a product manager at Wikimedia.

SpaceX

Founded in 2002 by entrepreneur Elon Musk, SpaceX has this vision:

> *SpaceX was founded under the belief that a future where humanity is out exploring the stars is fundamentally more exciting than one where we are not. Today SpaceX is actively developing the technologies to make this possible, with the ultimate goal of enabling human life on Mars.*

If your product vision includes the phrase "enabling human life on Mars," you qualify as ambitious.

Ancestry

Ancestry has a long history of helping people discover their genealogy, and in 2012 added their AncestryDNA service. Their story:

> Bringing together science and self-discovery, Ancestry helps everyone, everywhere discover the story of what led to them. Our sophisticated engineering and technology harnesses family history and consumer genomics ... to provide people with deeply meaningful insights about who they are and where they come from.

With the goal of providing people "insights about who they are and where they come from," it is easy to see why Ancestry entered the DNA testing service market—it was a natural (and necessary) extension to meet their vision.

Crafting a Vision

You'll want to craft a vision for your product. It might not be as lofty as helping all humans share in the sum of all knowledge, but your vision should be crisp, compelling, and motivating. Think about the core question: how, if you succeed, will the world be a better place?

Objectives

To track progress against your vision, you need specific, measurable goals—these are your objectives. If you were the product manager of Ancestry's DNA service or a similar service at 23andMe, your objectives might look something like the following:

1. Provide the world's most meaningful and insightful DNA service, as measured by customer satisfaction surveys
2. Be the worldwide market leader in ancestry DNA testing
3. Make more than $X million in annual profit

Our purpose as product managers is to manage products for customer delight, competitive advantage, and mouth-watering profitability. Your product objectives will link to these elements—customer satisfaction, market share, strengths vs. competitors, revenue growth, geographic expansion, upsell to higher value services, etc.

STRATEGY DIAMONDS

In 2005, Donald Hambrick and James Fredrickson wrote an excellent article, "Are you sure you have a strategy?" where they introduce the concept of strategy diamonds. My advice is to find the article, read it, and use it to guide your strategy discussions (step 5 above).

Hambrick and Fredrickson write about our sloppiness in using the term "strategy" —we use the term loosely and freely, with no depth. "Strategy has become a catchall term used to mean whatever one wants it to mean," they write. Most of what we call strategy is incomplete—just strategic elements or strategic threads.

If we are going to create winning product strategies, we need to be comprehensive in our thinking and include all the tangible elements of a strategy—not just bits and threads. The authors introduce the strategy diamond framework, and as product managers, we can use this structure to keep our thinking robust and comprehensive.

The strategy diamonds include the five elements of strategy: arenas, vehicles, differentiators, staging and pacing, and economic logic. Economic logic (or how we make money) is at the heart of the model, see Figure 4.2.

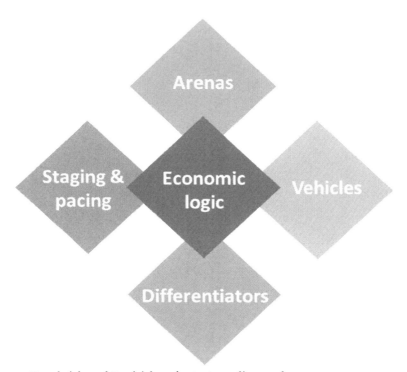

Figure 4.2: Hambrick and Fredrickson's strategy diamonds

As part of the ground-level work you do with your strategy team, you should step through each of these elements. I'll describe them below and include key questions in Figure 4.3.

Arenas

Sports teams play in arenas, and as part of our strategy work, we should articulate where our products play. We need to be as specific as possible. What is our product category, what market segments do we serve, and in what geographies do we operate? What are our core technologies? What customer needs do we meet? What, among all this, is changing over time? What opportunities are emerging?

Vehicles

As part of our strategy work, we define our market space (arenas) and then need to determine the capabilities to compete effectively in this space.

How we develop these capabilities is the focus of "vehicles" —it is what gets us there. What capabilities do we have today? What gaps do we have? How will we fill these gaps? Will we look at internal development, partnership, acquisition? For emerging market opportunities, how do we need to prepare?

Differentiators

Built into the very structure of our strategy work is competitive differentiation. What makes us different than our competitors? How are we better at meeting customer needs? How can we increase this competitive distance over time? How can we create near-permanent competitive differentiation? How will we win?

Staging and Pacing

If we have determined our market space (arenas), how we will acquire the required capabilities (vehicles), and how we can thump our competitors (differentiators), we need to figure out the sequence of our actions. What happens first, and what can happen later? As product managers, we instinctively know this area because we build and enhance our products in a stepwise fashion.

Staging and pacing requires forethought and prioritization. What gives us the biggest, earliest market win, while at the same time laying the groundwork for truly breakthrough products?

Economic Logic

At the heart of the strategy diamonds framework is economic logic— how we make profits and where we get our money. We need to spell out our business model, and given market trends and disruptive technology, how this will change over time. Economic logic is linked to all the other elements, for example, our choice and evolution of competitive differentiators.

Strategy diamonds analysis	
Arenas	What is our product category? What are our top market segments? What primary benefits do we provide to our customers? What geographies do we operate in? What are our core technologies? How is this changing over time? What market opportunities are emerging?
Vehicles	What capabilities do we have today to meet our objectives? What gaps do we have? How will we fill these gaps to meet our objectives and be successful in our chosen arena (e.g., internal development, partnership, acquisition)? What else do we need to do to prepare for emerging market opportunities?
Differentiators	What makes us better than competitors at meeting our customers' needs? How can we increase competitive distance over time?
Staging and pacing	To fill our gaps and meet our objectives, what specific steps will we take, and in what sequence? What will we do first, second, third? When will we do these? How can we sequence our steps to have early market wins, while laying the groundwork for breakthrough products and services?
Economic logic	What is our business model? How can we make money? How will this business model change through time?

Figure 4.3: Strategy diamonds analysis

Integrating All Five Elements

When you work with your strategy team, don't think of each of these areas discretely. An effective and coherent strategy for your product needs to integrate all these elements. For example, your choice of market segments and target customers should directly tie to an area you can generate competitive distance with. Doing this will, in turn, give you an opportunity to capture value and create healthy profits.

While I hope you sit in your cubicle and think deeply about an integrated strategy, this work happens best in a group, with diverse perspectives. You need to toss hypotheses around—debating, questioning, honing, and evolving your ideas. You are searching for a path that holds up well in front of your most skeptical colleagues and managers—and holds up well in a competitive market.

STRATEGY EXAMPLE: NAUTO, DRIVER SAFETY, AND AUTONOMOUS VEHICLES

Nauto was founded in 2015 in Palo Alto, California (the heart of Silicon Valley), and the company's core product helps make drivers safer. Nauto targets commercial transportation fleets and promotes a return on investment (ROI) of six months or less.

Drivers, safety managers, compliance managers, and CEOs all care deeply about safety. From a financial perspective, collisions—especially those that cause fatalities—can cost trucking and distribution firms millions of dollars. The costs come from vehicle damage, medical bills, reputation damage, lost business, fines and—in the worst-case scenarios—sky-high legal settlements.

From a personal perspective, a serious injury or loss of life can be horrific for all involved. Everyone in the transportation industry wants their drivers to get home safely and wants pedestrians and other drivers to walk away as if nothing happened—because nothing happened.

If you are a commercial fleet (e.g., a bus company or a long-haul trucking firm) and you sign up for Nauto's service, you will get a sophisticated bidirectional camera installed on the inside of your vehicle windshields. The external-facing lens sees the outside road, and the internal-facing lens sees the driver and passengers.

The cameras are always on, but only upload a video segment when there is safety "event." Hard braking and cornering will trigger a video. If the camera detects that the driver is looking away from the road for more than two and a half seconds, it will capture a video, and mark this as distracted driving. It also captures collisions.

Fleet managers then share these videos with drivers. Drivers rarely respond to data and graphs, but watching a video of themselves holding a mobile phone and nearly running a red light will cause positive changes.

Yes, But Why?

CEO Stefan Heck and his investors founded this company in 2015, and the underlying, perplexing question is "why?" The product is solid, and the return-on-investment is clear, but Nauto is a late entrant to the market, and two San Diego-based companies—Lytx and SmartDrive—dominate this market.

Nearly every major waste management company signed up for these services years ago (think large trucks, urban neighborhoods, and kids on bikes). The savings are so compelling that nearly all enterprise North American trucking and distribution firms have signed up as well. Contracts are for typically three to five years. If you were a sales representative for Nauto, you would quickly find that the most attractive companies already have dance partners.

To add challenges to this misery, drivers are going away. Waste management companies are experimenting with autonomous (driverless) trash and recycling pickup services. All major truck manufacturing firms are prototyping autonomous trucks. When the next five-year video safety contracts are ready for renewal, the industry will begin to feel downward pressure on the number of subscriptions. There simply won't be as many drivers to coach.

Why did Stefan Heck and his investors choose to enter this market? Why did they choose to play in this arena?

Building Toward Autonomous

We can use Hambrick and Fredrickson's strategy diamonds to make sense of Nauto, and the key is the interplay between "arenas" and "vehicles."

Let's think about the evolving transportation market—Nauto's chosen arena—in three overlapping and complex phases. The first phase (Arena 1) is drivers as we know them now: fully in charge of driving, with some assistance from adaptive cruise control, forward collision warnings, automatic emergency braking, etc.

In the second phase (Arena 2), vehicles take control of driving in less-challenging conditions, for example, long stretches on multi-lane highways. In this phase, drivers give control to the vehicle, but must be ready to take back control in challenging or unexpected conditions.

Vehicles are truly autonomous in the third phase (Arena 3), when people are passengers, but not drivers.

These three phases will be overlapping, with drivers, vehicle types, and road conditions all determining the level of autonomy. For example, well-marked and highly predictable multi-lane highways may see the first fully autonomous vehicles, while it will be many years before we see autonomous fuel trucks passing through Times Square in New York City.

If we start with Arena 1 (driving today), Nauto offers a bidirectional camera with uploaded video clips that help make commercial drivers safer. The spice of Nauto's strategy is that this product becomes a "vehicle" for Nauto to develop the skills for the second and third transportation phases (Arenas 2 and 3).

An example will make this clearer. Nauto currently uses the inside camera and artificial intelligence to detect if a driver is distracted, especially if the driver is looking down at a mobile phone. As Nauto builds their installed base of subscribers, they will get an increasing volume of data surrounding distraction—potentially millions of video clips of drivers looking down at their smartphones, or otherwise averting their eyes from the road. Using artificial intelligence, machine learning, and interaction with clients who are coaching drivers, Nauto will be able to refine and perfect their algorithms to ensure that they are truly capturing dangerous distracted driving (e.g., someone texting) while ignoring other "eyes off the road" scenarios (e.g., looking at rearview mirrors).

This avalanche of data will guide the product managers and engineers at Nauto to make their current product more valuable to trucking fleets—distracted driving is a major cause of collisions, and products that can prevent this have a strong return on investment. The result will be more subscription revenue, and an expanded installed base of fleets and drivers.

This data and learning will also prepare the company for the second phase of transportation's evolution when vehicles will drive autonomously on simpler road segments, while handing control back to humans in more complex situations.

In this second phase, the tough question is whether the driver is ready to take control. If the vehicle has been in autonomous mode, but suddenly finds itself lost with overhead signs and poor lane markings, can it successfully pass control back to the human in the driver seat?

As humans, we allow ourselves to be notoriously distracted and place unwarranted trust in new technology. We reach into the back seat to grab food from our backpacks; we put our laptops in the passenger seat and join WebEx meetings; we text, we play online games; sometimes we watch movies; sometimes we fall asleep.

Nauto's data surrounding distracted driving will provide the foundation for determining if a driver is ready to take control of a vehicle, or if they are simply too distracted (or too asleep). The algorithms Nauto is perfecting with facial recognition, head nod, and direction of eye gaze, will all guide its next-generation products to answer the question "is the human ready to drive?"

The volumes of data Nauto is collecting will also help guide the development of safe self-driving systems—the third phase of transportation evolution (Arena 3). Self-driving systems can manage the bulk of normal driving today, but there is a long tail of unique and perplexing driving conditions. We humans usually navigate these successfully, but they cause our machines to scratch their digital heads. A pedestrian is ready to step into an intersection, but waves for us to go first. An oncoming truck moves uphill toward us, on a curved mountain road with snow-covered lane markings. A construction worker is directing us to cross a double yellow line as a cement truck backs out.

As Nauto's data grows, the company will be able to use artificial intelligence and machine learning to understand how the best (and worst) drivers manage these long-tail traffic situations. This learning can then be used to refine self-driving systems. Nauto, through its strategy, is moving from a product that coaches drivers to a product that coaches algorithms.

Figure 4.4 maps out this strategy. Note how the learnings from a product in one arena become a vehicle to succeed in the next stage of market evolution.

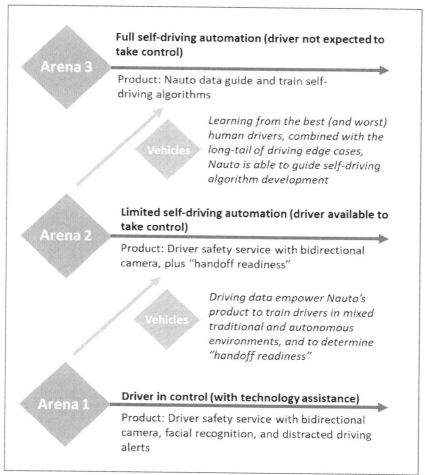

Figure 4.4: Nauto strategy example

Nauto: Key Takeaways

Nauto's product strategy will breathe and evolve, as all strategies should. As product managers, we can learn from Nauto's approach:

- Nauto recognized a disruptive technology (autonomous vehicles) and fully incorporated this market evolution into their strategy— not as a threat, but as an opportunity.

- Nauto's strategy actively uses Hambrick and Fredrickson's concept of "vehicles" —how the company can develop the capabilities to meet their objectives, how they can succeed in a world where machine learning, artificial intelligence, and algorithms are replacing drivers.
- The company's approach is holistic and integrated across all five strategic elements. Products in early arenas become vehicles to succeed as the market evolves. Subscription revenue from commercial fleets provides the economic logic and funds the collection of real-world driving data. With ever-growing volumes of data, Nauto creates competitive differentiators. The differentiators set Nauto up for further market success— generating greater volumes of data in a virtuous cycle. Staging and pacing is mapped over time, mirroring the evolution of autonomous driving.

DAY 4 FINAL WORDS

We talked earlier about the concept of return on investment (ROI). For us product managers, time spent creating, evolving, and enhancing a product strategy has some of the highest ROI of any work we do. Unfortunately, most product managers avoid strategy like it was next year's flu.

My advice: lean into product strategy. Gather a talented team, prepare a vision and objectives, and think holistically using the strategy diamonds framework. Together with your team—and their diverse perspectives— stretch, bend, and shape your strategy. Share a draft with your executives, tapping into their wisdom. Use this strategy to guide your roadmaps, your product development priorities, and your growth initiatives. Iterate over time. Go big and have an impact.

DAY 4 ON ONE PAGE

1. Most product managers **spend too little time** on strategy, limiting their impact on their products and their organizations. Strategy development is critical for customer delight, competitive advantage, and long-term profitability.

2. Product strategy is an integrated concept for **how we will meet our objectives**. Strategy guides product roadmaps, product development priorities, and where we find growth.

3. A product strategy **nests within**—and **complements**—a broader corporate strategy.

4. The **basic steps** for creating a strategy include: forming a cross-functional team; reviewing (or redoing) your market intelligence; crafting a vision and objectives; thinking and discussing; sharing and enhancing; and using and iterating.

5. A **product vision** articulates how the world will be a better place if we succeed. It should be compelling, motivating, and ambitious. **Objectives** are the specific, measurable goals we can use to track progress against our vision.

6. Hambrick and Fredrickson's **strategy diamonds** provide a framework for us to be comprehensive and thorough. The five strategic elements are arenas, vehicles, differentiators, staging and pacing, and economic logic.

7. Key to an effective strategy is the **integration of the five strategic elements**. The Palo Alto-based Nauto provides a good example of a well-considered approach that—in the face of a disruptive technology—integrates all the strategy elements, with a focus on the interplay of arenas and vehicles.

DAY 5: PRIORITIZATION AND ROADMAPPING

Focusing on the Breakthrough, Tuning Out the Noise

Companies can, and often do, run into trouble with development priorities, and struggle to get new and compelling products out the door.

One of the key dangers is constant strategy changes. If it takes your development team six months to get major upgrades into the market, but your strategy changes every four months, you will never make it. You'll be frustrated, your engineers will lose motivation, and your customers will still be working with the same, semi-functioning product.

A second danger, especially for business-to-business products and services, is death by a thousand requests. You meet with managers from a key enterprise client in Green Bay, Wisconsin, and they (very politely) present you with a spreadsheet of twenty-six upgrades to your service they would like to see. Next to each of the requests is a column listing the "expected completion" date. You've seen this before, and they want to know the status.

The following week, you meet with a client in Calgary, Alberta, and receive fourteen additional requests. Later, at a meeting with your Korean sales team, you are given another list of changes needed to win a very large deal with one of the Samsung companies.

Most of these requests share two properties: 1) they are valuable to a particular client, but nearly worthless to others, and 2) they take significant bandwidth from your development team, diverting them from creating truly breakthrough products.

A third danger is overly long and bureaucratic planning cycles. You do research, you go through gate reviews, you sync development schedules with complementary products, and you do additional reviews. You finally launch the product one and a half years after your original proposal, only to find the market has changed.

These are common issues, unfortunately. Step into any technology company, and you are more likely to find underperforming product development groups than to find those delivering innovative, market-leading products.

Development teams sometimes have the instincts to develop stellar products without us product managers, but more typically development teams weave, bob, and meander without good prioritization and guidance. They shift their development priorities to support the CEO's favorite project, they overreact to loud clients, and they patch databases and build technical debt. They know where true innovation lies, but they just can't get there.

The good news is that we, as product managers, can help. We work side-by-side with our development teams and prioritize development work. Using our market intelligence and product strategy, we steer development efforts to create products with customer delight, competitive advantage, and healthy profitability. If you want to have a long-term impact as a product manager, focus on prioritization.

In the following sections, we'll talk through three processes to help guide development efforts:
- Objectives and key results (OKRs)
- Development buckets
- Roadmapping

OKRs convert our big-picture strategy to this quarter's goals. Development buckets can help manage the myriad of enhancement requests and focus on true innovation. Roadmapping charts our strategy over time and builds a shared understanding of our path forward.

OBJECTIVES AND KEY RESULTS (OKRS)

In our Day 4 discussion, we talked about crafting a product vision and strategy, thus setting a product path for one to five years. OKRs convert this big-picture vision and product strategy into tangible quarterly goals.

OKRs are used by some of our best product management companies, including Google (which pioneered the concept), LinkedIn, and Netflix.

As product managers, we want to focus on the *big impact* items—the areas of innovation that motivate our customers and discourage our competitors. An OKR process, managed jointly with our engineering counterparts, can help us focus on the right projects and sidestep the near-constant distractions.

The "objectives" portion of the OKRs state the business goal, and the "key results" give measurable outcomes that can be used later to grade achievement.

Let's assume we are product managers for a service that helps medical facilities track compliance versus government regulations. As part of our strategy, we want to enhance the core value of our product, which is to keep our clients out of regulatory trouble and save patient lives. For the third quarter, we want to make it easier for clients to assess their risk of government fines and patient lawsuits. With this we can craft our first objective (see Figure 5.1).

OKRs for Q3	Score
Objective 1: Enhance a hospital's ability to assess its risk of government fines or patient lawsuits	**0.7**
Key results — Reduce clicks by 75% to access key compliance indicators	1.0
Release enhancements to five beta customers by end of Q3	0.4

Figure 5.1: OKR example

Associated with this objective are measurable key results. In our example, we want to reduce the number of clicks required to see key compliance indicators. We also want to release our enhancements to five beta clients by the end of the quarter.

Note that the "how" (dashboards, risk meters, reports, etc.) is not included in the OKR, we are focused on business goals and client outcomes. The details of how we do this will evolve in the "discovery and delivery" phase, which we'll describe in our Day 6 discussion.

In the example OKR above (Figure 5.1), we have included the scores, but these only appear when we grade ourselves at the end of a quarter. If we follow Google's approach, scores are between zero and one. In the example, we succeeded in reducing clicks by 75%, so we give ourselves a "1." However, we only released our enhancements to two of five beta clients, so we score this at "0.4." The overall score for the objective is a simple average of the key results, in this case, "0.7."

Although it sounds counterintuitive, a score of around 0.7 is optimal. Why don't we strive for 1? We want to meet our objectives fully, but we also want to push the product envelope. If we are consistently getting scores of 1, we are not aggressive enough when we write our OKRs. The OKRs should feel ambitious, and a little uncomfortable. They should feel like a stretch.

OKR Process

There are four basic steps to creating, using, and scoring OKRs.

1) Create two or three OKRs each quarter, with business outcomes as objectives, and measurable key results. You can create OKRs at a company, group, and personal level, but for our purposes, you should define OKRs for your product team. Focus on the big impact items—the areas of development that will push your product forward, make it more innovative, please your customers, increase competitive distance, and enhance your profitability. Don't include all the monthly or quarterly run-rate tasks in your OKRs. Create these OKRs together with your development team leads.

2) Share your OKRs with your executive and management teams to ensure consensus. Modify based on their feedback.

3) Use your OKRs to tightly focus development efforts. Make sure your product team members (engineers, user experience designers, data analysts, etc.) are aware of the OKRs, and internalize these as goals.

4) Review and score your OKRs with your product team and executives at the end of each quarter. If you hit 1 with your objectives, quietly smile at yourself in the mirror, but be more aggressive in your goal setting for the following quarter. If your scores are low, determine the reason behind this, and make any needed adjustments.

OKRs are a strong tool for us to steer product development efforts toward a strategy, and toward a product vision. OKRs also empower a product team—we aren't defining the "how," but rather spelling out a business opportunity for a team to solve.

DEVELOPMENT BUCKETS

It is rare for development teams to be able to spend 100% of their time on high-impact items. Often our teams have other demands—customer enhancement requests, technical support escalations, operations, etc. These "other" demands can often overwhelm development teams, leaving little bandwidth for innovation. New products and breakthrough enhancements often get neglected in the rush to meet urgent, tactical needs.

Development buckets are an effective tool to prioritize your engineering efforts. Start by categorizing the various areas of product development work. With a product group I worked with recently, the areas were: big impact items (innovation and breakthroughs), near-term client enhancement requests (from our largest customers), support and bug fixes, operational support (like monthly billing), and technical debt (improving performance and fixing past shortcuts). Place these categories in the left column of a chart (see Figure 5.2).

Development category	Percentage of development time	Items
Big impact items	65%	Use your OKRs to prioritize these items
Near-term client enhancement requests	10%	Item 1 Item 2 Item 3 *In priority order*
Support and bug fixes	10%	Item 1 Item 2 Item 3 *In priority order*
Operational support	5%	Item 1 Item 2 Item 3 *In priority order*
Technical debt	10%	Item 1 Item 2 Item 3 *In priority order*

Figure 5.2: Development buckets

Now determine, together with your engineering managers, how much time you will spend on each bucket. Reserve as much time as possible for the "big impact items"—those areas that are key to your longer-term strategy. If you are working within an Agile software development environment, you can use the Agile concept of "points" to gauge (and guide) efforts in each of these categories.

In the following column, list all the items that need development work, in top-to-bottom priority. For the "big impact items," your OKRs will guide the list. For the items in the other buckets, work with your extended team to determine which are the highest priorities.

You can then use this list to guide your development efforts. Instruct your engineering teams to work on these items, starting from the top and working down the list, constrained by the time percentages.

This technique is not complex, it's not rocket science. And, it helps us in a few strong ways:

1. *Faster, streamlined prioritization of development efforts:* Once we set the top-level percentages by category (e.g., 10% for client enhancement requests and 5% for operational support) we can focus on prioritizing items within each bucket, but not between buckets. It's nearly impossible to prioritize specific items in different categories (e.g., is a loud request from a key enterprise account more important than a smoother billing process?). It is much easier to prioritize within a bucket, for example, stack-ranking all bug fixes.

2. *More development team independence:* With clear priorities, development teams can work down the lists within these buckets, with minimal help from us.

3. *Greater focus on big impact items:* Focus is the bright star of development buckets. With this simple tool, we can quickly transition scattered and ineffective product development efforts into one that delivers innovative, breakthrough products. Working with various product teams, I've seen this transition happen within three to six months.

ROADMAPPING

Roadmapping is a third tool (after OKRs and development buckets) for us product managers to steer, guide and prioritize development efforts.

Unlike OKRs and development buckets, roadmaps are controversial. They can help clarify a product strategy over time, and force important tradeoffs, but they can also be unrealistic and create wasted work. From my own experience, roadmaps run the gamut from helpful to misguided.

In this section, we'll talk about how to use roadmaps successfully, and how to avoid the traps.

The What, the Why and the Dangers

Roadmaps are time-based charts showing the planned evolution of a product or service. They are a visual tool that you can share with your development teams, managers, and executives, and unite them on a common path. They clarify a product direction in ways that strategy documents, stack-ranked feature charts, and fuzzy Agile processes can't.

Roadmaps can also force tradeoffs. Product management expert Rich Mironov talks about how marketing and sales teams live in an "and" world, that is, "we can do this *and* this." Engineering lives in an "exclusive/or" world, that is, "we can either do this *or* this." A roadmapping process helps us step away from the unrealistic "and" world, and can force healthy tradeoffs between competing features and opportunities. "If we develop X feature this quarter, we will need to move Y feature to next quarter. Is this acceptable?"

There are dangers with roadmaps, however. Marty Cagan, with a healthy dose of consultant hyperbole, states that "roadmaps are the root of so much evil." Here are the problems:

1) *Wasted work:* Roadmaps can create unnecessary work, violating lean principles. If we detail features over six months or a year (or longer) with our roadmaps, we run the risk that new learnings from the market will make our work irrelevant. If our engineers have started working on unnecessary roadmap features, we have created even more waste. "At least half of the items on your roadmap are never going to work with customers," states Cagan.

2) *Unrealistic timelines:* For the vast majority of roadmaps, we are hopelessly optimistic. We think we can complete a major product refresh by the end of the year, but we are off by six months or more. We expect to develop five major, new features, but only have engineering bandwidth for two.

3) *Roadmaps as commitments:* When we share roadmaps with executives, they will often take these as commitments, even with all our disclaimers. Roadmaps that are communicated, but missed, can cause confusion and tension in the organization. Why can't our product teams deliver on time?

4) *Premature communication with customers:* Sales teams may share early roadmaps with clients to help win deals. The features, products, and timelines of these roadmaps frequently change, however, and clients expecting a major product refresh by the end of the year won't be happy when it doesn't happen.

If you decide to use roadmaps, my advice is to use them to visualize your longer-term strategy, without detailing features. You should expect specific features to evolve and morph through the discovery and delivery process (Day 6), and because of this, you don't want to detail features that will soon change—especially if your sales teams and executives will view these as commitments.

Also, don't get caught in the trap of doing roadmaps yourself. Roadmaps need to be a collaborative effort between yourself and your engineering leads. Collectively you have the credibility that you won't have if you are working on your own.

Finally, sanitize and conservatize anything shared with customers and prospects. You may need two versions of your roadmap—one for you and your development team, and a much fuzzier, timeline-stretched version for key clients.

Creating Roadmaps

Energetic product managers and their teams have developed many flavors of roadmaps over the years: single product roadmaps, product family roadmaps, technology roadmaps, etc. If you are using your roadmaps to illustrate your strategy, a format that encompasses technology, products, and markets is useful. See Figure 5.3 below.

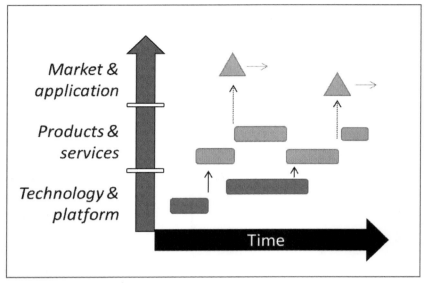

Figure 5.3: Roadmap example

The x-axis is time, and this can be in months, quarters or years.

On the y-axis, we start with "technology and platform." I worked at HP for many years, as a worldwide and regional product manager for color laser printers. Our "technology and platform" was a printer engine and toner cartridge that we co-developed with Canon.

Next up on the y-axis: is "products and services." On HP roadmaps, we might use a printer engine (the "platform"), and develop a printer for small businesses. We might also develop a second product off the same platform by adding scanning and copying capabilities to make a multifunction printer.

The products we develop off platforms or technology may, in turn, allow us to reach new markets. In the HP example, the new color laser printers may allow us to target small businesses wanting to print their marketing materials for tradeshows, or for in-store signage.

This format is one of many viable approaches: you'll have to determine a style that is most effective with your products and your organization.

You can use Microsoft Office tools like PowerPoint or Excel to create roadmaps, but increasingly there are excellent tools included with product management software, like Aha! and ProductPlan.

PRIORITIZATION–AN EXAMPLE

I recently worked with a small U.S. technology company running into a buzz saw of strategy and prioritization issues. The team had a very effective product manager during the proceeding couple of years, but he had moved to other opportunities, and the company had been without a full-time product manager for six months.

As with many technology markets, this company's arena was evolving rapidly, driven by a combination of technology advancement and regulatory change. The company's product had high potential, but clients were drifting away, and future revenue projections were not pleasant.

The engineering team consisted of a small set of top-notch engineers, with long market experience and strong empathy for their customers. The team's full bandwidth was absorbed by responding to client customization requests, connecting to new partners, and managing the ongoing operations.

The engineering leadership desperately wanted to create breakthrough, next-generation products that would match the new regulatory requirements and reinvigorate the company's value proposition. They were frustrated, however, that they couldn't find the time to do this.

Fortunately, this story has a happy ending. We followed the recipe I've outlined over the past few days. We started with ethnographic research— talking with clients over the phone and at their sites. The insights gained from this research helped fuel a concurrent strategy process, where we worked with our executive team to recommend the best path forward.

Once we had a draft strategy in place, we used this to develop quarterly OKRs—with one OKR focused on meeting the new regulatory requirements, and second on refreshing the look, feel, and usability of our product. We used development buckets to ensure we put more than 60% of our development bandwidth toward these two OKRs. We actively limited work on client customization requests and bug fixes, while reserving some space to reduce technical debt and improve performance. We also crafted a roadmap that reflected our strategy, but didn't go into restrictive depth.

The team met the regulatory deadlines, and the product refresh was well-received by existing clients. The clearer value proposition of the new product helped the sales team sign one of the biggest new clients in the company's history. Revenue projections became a lot more pleasant.

I'll note two takeaways from this example. First, if you want to develop market-leading products, prioritization matters. OKRs and development buckets are key tools. Second, as product managers, we lead prioritization, but it takes a receptive and engaged product team to make this happen. Fortunately, most engineering teams welcome this type of work: they want to develop products that thrill customers, punch competitors, and make big chunks of profit.

DAY 5 FINAL WORDS

Skillfully prioritizing development efforts is key to becoming a more strategic product manager; in fact, it is one of the fastest ways for us to get runs on the board.

OKRs, development buckets, and roadmaps all can help. Objectives and key results are a strong and proven tool for converting big-picture vision and strategy into this quarter's development goals. Development buckets can help your engineering team focus on the big impact items, tuning out the noise. Roadmaps can get you into trouble, but if you sidestep the traps, they can help visualize a strategy and manage tradeoffs.

Do all this prioritization work with skill, and you'll earn enthusiastic high-fives from your customers, and grudging grief from your competitors.

DAY 5 ON ONE PAGE

1. Technology companies often run into trouble with **development priorities** and struggle to get new and compelling products into the market.

2. **Key dangers** include constant strategy changes, death by a thousand requests, and long, overly bureaucratic planning cycles.

3. Prioritizing product development efforts is one of our most important jobs as strategically minded product managers. We can add **significant value** here.

4. **Objectives and key results** (OKRs) are an approach used by some of our best product management companies (Google, LinkedIn, Netflix) to convert a longer-term vision and strategy into this quarter's development objectives.

5. **Development buckets** are a simple tool to focus our engineering efforts on the areas with the greatest impact, while avoiding the myriad of near-term distractions.

6. **Roadmaps** as a tool have both power and danger for product managers. They can help visualize and communicate a product strategy, and force healthy tradeoffs. If they are too detailed and prescriptive, however, they can create wasted work and generate unrealistic expectations.

DAY 6: DISCOVERY AND DELIVERY

The Art of Ooching

In one of the opening scenes of the Netflix original series *Stranger Things*, four middle-school boys—Mike, Dustin, Lucas, and Will—are in Mike's basement playing a wild game of Dungeons & Dragons. The boys have just encountered the bone-chilling monster, Demogorgon, when Mike's mother insists it is time for everyone to go home. Will, on the bike ride back to his house, enters a path through a dark-forested road and encounters a real-life (or at least movie-life) Demogorgon, setting the stage for a season one show that mirrors an intense Dungeons & Dragons game.

Ernest Gygax and David Arneson developed Dungeons & Dragons in the early 1970s. The game became immensely popular in the late 1970s and early 1980s, and more than thirty million people have played the Dungeons & Dragons since its inception.

The early versions of Dungeons & Dragons included a host of innovations: a narrative role-playing game, with persistent characters each seeking adventure in a fantasy landscape, looking to gain experience, knowledge, and power. If this sounds familiar today—and it should—then give credit to Dungeons & Dragons for influencing a whole generation of video games that were to follow it.

Gygax and Arneson would have never considered themselves product managers, but even the best among us could learn from them. The team started with a wealth of ideas and innovations and then went through a rigorous experimentation process—expanding on some ideas, and dropping others. Gygax first tested the game with his eleven-year-old son and nine-year-old daughter, and then with his local gamer friends. Arneson started a separate group. Both tested the game at clubs and conventions, with frequent back-and-forth discussions: What's working? What's not working? What should we change?

Based on hundreds (maybe thousands) of experimental games, Gygax and Arneson rewrote the rules and reran the sessions. Eventually, they published the game, only to find they needed more role-playing guidance for new players who hadn't experienced firsthand the enthusiasm of Arneson and Gygax. The team started a newsletter giving examples of how to create your own adventures, and clarifying rules around spells, creatures, and magical items. In the years since, the experiments, learning, and revisions—sourced from a creative set of users—have never stopped.

The creation and evolution of Dungeons & Dragons followed a discovery and delivery product management best practice. Gygax and Arneson didn't write an innovative game and toss it to the market. Instead, they had a full set of creative ideas that went through a continuous experimentation and discovery process. In a series of incremental releases, they delivered versions of this game to a narrow—and then increasingly broad—set of gamers. Even after releasing to the full market, they continued to get feedback—modifying the rules and expanding the game.

Discovery and delivery, well executed by Gygax and Arneson, is the subject of our Day 6 discussion.

DISCOVERY AND DELIVERY

Let's start with an observation—our product enhancement ideas run the gamut from the excellent to the utterly worthless. This is normal, in fact completely healthy. The trick is to winnow our ideas in a fast and low-cost way, and only develop those ideas we have high confidence of market fit.

A product management best practice is to use a discovery and delivery process. The basic concept is to take ideas for new and enhanced products from multiple sources, and quickly get these in front of customers for feedback. For ideas that are testing well, deliver these to the market in fast, incremental releases.

Who leads a discovery and delivery process? The short answer is you, the product manager. We don't do this alone, however. In fact, for technology companies there is magic in a three-person team—an engineering lead, a user experience (UX) lead, and a product manager (you).

Figure 6.1 illustrates the discovery and delivery process. On the x-axis is product readiness—from rough to refined, from sketched prototypes to scalable products. On the y-axis is market fit—from uncertain to high, from ideas that might be awful to those we know will make the grade.

In the following sections, we'll step through each of the four steps.

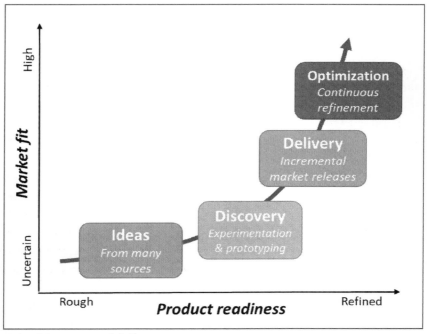

Figure 6.1: Discovery and delivery process

Ideas

As part of a discovery and delivery process, we source ideas from many different places:

- *Engineering teams:* Our engineering teams have the best knowledge of what technology is just now enabling, and this is a rich source of new product ideas. In fact, for technology companies, this is one of our richest sources.
- *Ethnographic research:* A deep, intuitive understanding of our customers and their needs (discussed in Day 2) is probably the second richest fount of ideas for new products and enhancements.
- *Product usage data:* The data surrounding our products and their usage provide guidance for product enhancements. If you are working with software, it is relatively straightforward to instrument your product, track where users go, where they get stuck, and what areas of your product they avoid like a foot rash. Product usage

data is a rich and honest source of insights to guide your next-generation development.

- *Executives:* As product managers, we grumble about executives stopping by our desk with their favorite product ideas. In my own experience, some of these ideas are off-track while others come from deep market understanding (CEOs and founders are often the original product managers in a company). The joy of a discovery and delivery process is that we can test our executives' ideas with customers, keeping those with strong market fit, and justifiably bypassing those that don't test well.
- *Sales and account teams:* Sales and client service teams are a common source of new product enhancement ideas. We should recognize an inherent bias, however, especially with enterprise sales teams. To quote Rich Mironov, "customer-facing groups deal with the world one account at a time, while product folks and development organizations deal with customer segments as a whole." Ideas from sales teams may be generalized from one major account, but "we don't want to build products one account at a time."
- *Competitors:* As discussed in Day 3, competitors often scoop us with good product ideas. If you can, shamelessly cherry-pick the best ideas, and consider them for your product.

Of the full list, engineering teams, ethnographic research, and product usage data are probably the most important. Start here, and you'll be in good shape.

Discovery

Experimentation, testing, and prototyping are the keys to "discovery." The goal is to quickly (and inexpensively) vet ideas with potential customers. Our goal is to "discover" reality rather than predict it.

We start with the lowest cost of all prototypes—maybe just a PowerPoint mockup that you share with potential clients for feedback. The ethnographic research we talked about on Day 2 is a great opportunity to get feedback on new concepts.

As ideas evolve and get more traction, we move to more advanced representations—3D printouts, clickable prototypes, etc. In this process, we want fast, dense client feedback to help steer a product's evolution, while at the same time minimizing time and cost from our development team.

Chip and Dan Heath, in their book *Decisive*, use the term "ooch"—constructing small experiments to test your hypothesis, working toward deeper knowledge with small, low-risk steps. "We always ooch before we leap." (I love this word!) Discovery is simply ooching in a product development context.

Marty Cagan suggests focusing on four key risks during the discovery phase:

1. *Value risk:* Does our idea have customer value? Will they pay for it?
2. *Usability risk:* Can our users figure out how to use it?
3. *Feasibility risk:* Can we develop this? Do we have the skills and time?
4. *Stakeholder risk:* Is our management supportive of our direction?

Through the ooching process, we discard ideas that aren't working, and we hone, refine, and evolve the ones that are showing promise. When we are ready for a product enhancement to move to the "delivery" phase, and get developed (for real, at scale), we can be confident that we are asking our engineers to develop new products and enhancements with true product-market fit. This is lean product management and lean product development.

Delivery

When new products, features, or enhancements have moved through discovery, and we know there is a good match between the market, company strategy, and technology, it's time to release these capabilities to our customers.

A series of incremental releases—smaller and sooner—is usually preferable to holding back functionality to wait for a more complete release later. Incremental releases allow us to get new value in the hands of our customers sooner, get market feedback faster, and course-correct earlier if we have missed the mark.

From my experience working with various teams, product managers often make mistakes here. They draw a circle around a set of functionality and call this the "minimum viable product" (MVP). This set of functionality—the MVP—is drawn too expansively, however, and takes time to develop. The results are not always happy, with delayed customer value, postponed market feedback, and slow product evolution.

There is controversy about MVPs, but my advice is to think Agile, to think lean, and focus more on the "minimum" as opposed to the "viable." For most products (especially software), smaller and sooner is better than bigger and later.

Optimization

Many development efforts are never finished, and as more formerly hardware-based products become increasingly software based (think autonomous vehicles), this will just become more true. All trends point toward a market and technology environment where we are continuously optimizing our products.

From discovery to delivery to optimization, we are moving from narrow market feedback (prototypes) to broader customer feedback (beta programs) to full market feedback (released products). We use product usage data, customer support input, social media forums, etc. to gauge reaction to our products and generate ideas for further optimization—and for new enhancements and new product ideas that will get fed back into the discovery and delivery process.

Discovery and Delivery as a Funnel

With the discovery and delivery model, we work with a large set of ideas at the beginning and narrow the list as we go (see Figure 6.2).

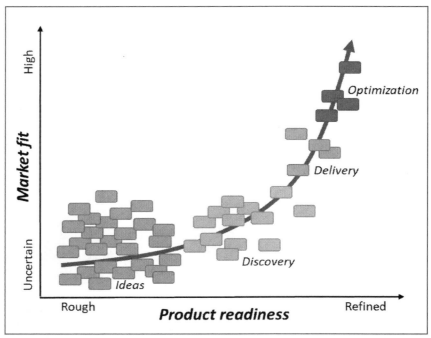

Figure 6.2: Discovery and delivery as a funnel

We know that some of these ideas are excellent, some are mediocre, and some are yawn-inducing—we just don't know which are which. During the discovery phase, we test our ideas and discard those that are not showing value. For those demonstrating market fit, we continue to modify and refine them—honing their customer value and strengthening their competitive advantage.

In the delivery phase—when we ask our engineers to develop these ideas in a way that is robust, scalable, and manufacturable—we are down to a small set. We focus our engineering efforts on ideas with solid product-market fit, reducing wasted work on blasé enhancements.

Concurrent and Parallel

When we are looking at a broader set of enhancements, features, and new products, much of our work across the four discovery and delivery phases happens concurrently, and in parallel (see Figure 6.3, and note that the x-axis has been changed to time).

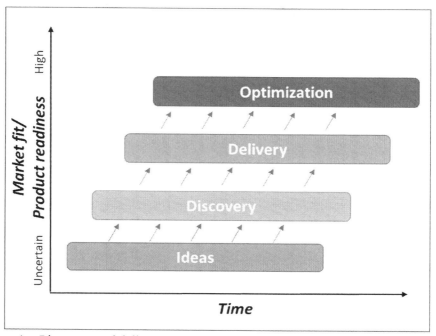

Figure 6.3: Discovery and delivery process—concurrent and parallel

We are continually getting new ideas from the market, and testing prototypes with customers. When we feel confident we have winning ideas, we pass these along to get developed, and once the products are in the market, we optimize them and use these as a source for new ideas.

In other words, this is not a waterfall method. We don't gather all ideas and then test them all at once in a discovery phase. We don't pass winning ideas *en masse* to a delivery phase. Discovery and delivery is an Agile and lean process: we peel off winning ideas when we find them, and push them through the process. The result is fast, incremental enhancements and fast product evolution.

STAGE-GATES

Discovery and delivery offers a compelling approach to new product development, and some of the world's best product companies use versions of this method: Amazon, Google, LinkedIn, Netflix, and Facebook. However, most technology companies worldwide use a different method, i.e., some form of waterfall or "stage-gates," interspersed with Agile software development.

I hesitate to use the term "waterfall" because it has become taboo among the product development community—shorthand for slow, cumbersome, and overly bureaucratic. Consultant Marty Cagan talks (and writes) at length about waterfall methods as the "root cause of product failure." Keep an open mind however, waterfall methods are appropriate for some products, while being uncompetitive and dangerous for others.

One of the best-articulated approaches for product development—with a hardware and waterfall heritage—is Robert Cooper and Scott Edgett's stage-gate process.

Stage-gates are an organized, manageable process from idea to launch. The "stages" are phases of new product or service development, for example: scoping, business case, development, testing, and launch. The "gates" are management checkpoints where product development is reviewed, managers make go/kill decisions, and resources are approved (or not) for the next stage. See Figure 6.4.

Figure 6.4: Stage-gates

The rapid prototyping of the discovery and delivery model can (and should) be incorporated into the various stages. Cooper and Edgett use the term "spiral development" for this.

The "scoping" stage incorporates ethnographic research, with active listening and observation, followed by concept testing with simple prototypes (maybe just a PowerPoint mockup). During the "business case" stage, prototypes are honed and refined, with repeated customer feedback loops (spirals). In the "development" stage, product managers and engineers share components of actual products with customers, gaining deeper feedback. When the products are fully developed, beta tests provide customer feedback, and we get broad market feedback as we move into the "launch" phase.

Discovery and Delivery vs. Stage-Gates

Discovery and delivery methods have a software, Agile, and lean product development heritage (think Google, LinkedIn, and Netflix), while stage-gates evolved from more hardware-centric, waterfall methods (think GE industrial equipment, HP printers, and NASA space missions). Discovery and delivery methods are fast, flexible, highly responsive to the market, and can be jaw-droppingly productive. Stage-gates are systematic, careful, deliberate, and can be slow.

	Discovery & delivery	Stage-gates
Heritage	Lean, Agile, software	Waterfall, hardware
Characteristics	Flexible, fast, highly productive	Systematic, deliberate, can be slow
Market requirements	Concurrent (or closely prior) to development work	Prior to development work
Sweet spot	Rapid software development	High investment hardware development
Risks	Poor coordination and financial risk with complex projects	Getting swamped by faster discovery and delivery competitors

Figure 6.5: Discovery and delivery compared to stage-gates

Market requirements are often determined concurrently (or closely before) development work with discovery and delivery. There is often a longer gap between market understanding and development work with stage-gate approaches, and this can cause issues in quickly evolving markets. Products can be launched with an unimpressive thud when market research and product development are separated by a year or more.

The sweet spot of discovery and delivery methods are rapid software development and markets moving at light speed—gaming, online retail, social media. For stage-gates, the sweet spot leans toward hardware, where projects require high investment, and mistakes can be very expensive—

G.E. power turbines, multi-cable transit boxes on nuclear submarines, NASA missions to Mars.

Both models carry risks. Coordination across multiple groups with complex projects is tough with a discovery and delivery approach. Companies using stage-gate methods run the risk of getting swamped by faster, more nimble discovery and delivery competitors—and this is where we, as product managers, should worry.

My advice: if your company is primarily using waterfall, stage-gate approaches, start infusing more discovery and delivery methods. Step out with your engineering leads and user experience managers, meet your customers (and competitors' customers and non-users). Incorporate their feedback into rapid-release product development. Lather, rinse, and repeat.

The winners in competitive markets are often not the companies with the best initial ideas, but those companies with the fastest product evolution.

DAY 6 FINAL WORDS

Gygax and Arneson, when they created Dungeons & Dragons, went through an impressive discovery and delivery process.

They started with a broad set of innovations and ideas—sourced from other gamers, fantasy literature, and their own creativity—and crafted a prototype game. Then Gygax and Arneson did what we should do with our own ideas, they went to their customers and tried it out. They played this game with their kids, their friends, and conventions full of nerdy gamers. They changed the rules, they reran their sessions, they ooched—always evolving, enhancing, and improving their product. This work didn't stop after they published the game—Gygax and Arneson continued to gather feedback, extend the game, and enhance the rules.

Most of us won't work on products that inspire a Netflix series (none of mine have), but we can all incorporate experimentation, learning, and ooching with the goal of rapid product evolution, customer delight, competitive advantage, and more than our fair share of profits.

DAY 6 ON ONE PAGE

1. Our **product enhancement ideas** run the gamut from the excellent to the utterly worthless, and this is normal and healthy. Our job is to winnow these ideas in a fast and low-cost way, keeping those with high market fit, and discarding the rest.

2. A well-run **discovery and delivery** process is a product management best practice. We take ideas from multiple sources and quickly get them in front of customers for feedback. For ideas that are testing well, we deliver these to the market in fast, incremental releases.

3. As product managers, we lead the discovery and delivery process, but we should run this process together with a small, core team. There is magic in the **combined perspectives** of an engineering lead, a user experience (UX) designer, and a product manager.

4. There are four basic steps in the discovery and delivery process: **ideas, discovery, delivery, and optimization**. The work between these areas is less sequential and more concurrent and interactive. We start with multiple ideas, but only ask our development team to finalize those with customer value, solid usability, feasible technology, and benefit for our company.

5. **Stage-gates** represent an alternative development model and can be appropriate for complex projects with high investment, where mistakes can be difficult and expensive to correct.

6. Winners in competitive markets are often not those with the best initial ideas, but those with the **fastest product evolution**.

DAY 7: PRICING

Our New Best Friend

If we plotted the various work of product management, with *time spent* on the x-axis, and *value to business* on the y-axis, pricing—for most product managers—would fall into the "huge value, don't spend much time there" part of the graph.

This is unfortunate since the impact of systematic pricing analysis can be enormous for the company's profitability. It's one of the top areas, we as product managers, can have an impact on our companies. If you are responsible for pricing, this is an area to lean into, this is an area to say an emphatic "yes" to.

WHY PRICING IS IMPORTANT

Our purpose as product managers is to manage the full lifecycle of products and services to create exceptional customer value, generate a long-term competitive advantage, and deliver year-after-year profitability. If we put a mental circle around the word "profitability"—pricing can be the fastest and most effective way to increase our margins, to increase profits coming in the door. Pricing should be our new best friend.

Let's talk through a simple example to illustrate why pricing is so important. Let's say the price of one of our products is €100, and we have fixed costs of €25 and variable costs of €66. In this stick-figure example, our operating profit is €9.

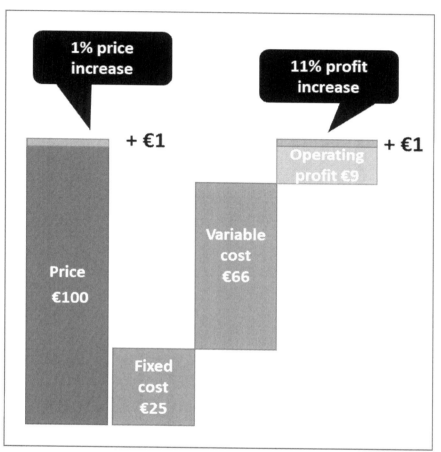

Figure 7.1: Impact of a 1% price increase

If we increase the price by €1 (a small 1% price change), we increase our operating profit by 11% (a big, eyebrow-raising jump). If, as an alternative, we spent time with our executives and accounting team and manage to reduce fixed costs by 1% for our product, our operating profit would increase by less than 3%. Reducing variable costs—no easy task—would have a slightly greater impact on profit, but still far below the 11% improvement triggered by a 1% change in price.

Pricing, at the end of a long product management day, is one of the fastest and easiest ways to increase profitability.

WHY PRICING IS HARD FOR PRODUCT MANAGERS

Many of us product managers avoid pricing like it was something a stray dog left behind—we take care of it when we need to, but otherwise look the other way. There are at least two reasons for this: pricing can entail a brain-numbing level of detail (it's rare that we can change one top-level price and be done); and pricing is controversial, it's conflict rich.

We'll talk about pricing detail later, but let's think about the contentious nature of setting prices.

As product managers, we sit in and among many groups, and through our work we serve multiple masters. We work with sales managers, who are interested in securing a deal and meeting this quarter's targets. They want pricing—or special discounts—to ensure they can do this. We work with our marketing teams, and they want to optimize product positioning, within a product line and versus competitors—and pricing is a key component of this. Our finance managers want healthy profits. CEOs want all these things, but often have a bias toward market leadership and share. See Figure 7.2.

Figure 7.2: Why pricing is hard for product managers

As product managers, we need to manage all these competing objectives, which is no simple task. Pricing challenges both our analytic and people skills.

THE 3CS OF PRICING

When you are pricing your product, it helps to think first of the outer boundaries: the lowest and highest possible prices.

We typically don't want to sell at a price below our cost of providing the product or service. We would have no profit if we priced this way. "Cost of product" is the first of pricing's three Cs.

On the other extreme, we usually cannot price higher than the value customers derive from our product. Why would they purchase our product if the price exceeds the benefits? If we priced this high, we'd have no demand. "Customer value" is the second C.

We don't sell our products inside walled gardens, and in well-functioning markets there are competing products and services that provide alternatives for our customers. "Competitive environment" is the third C. Refer to Figure 7.3.

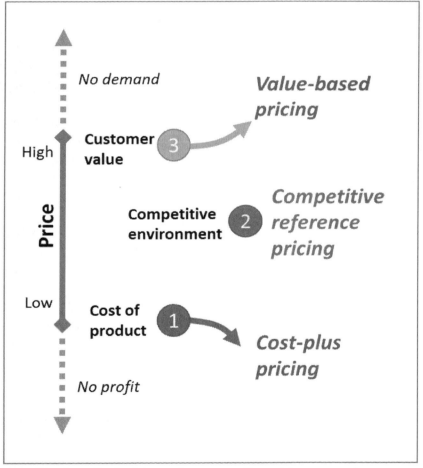

Figure 7.3: The three Cs of pricing and corresponding pricing approaches

PRICING APPROACHES

Each of these three Cs links to a different pricing approach. Let's spell them out.

Cost-plus pricing: **For companies that focus on the cost of a product as their primary reference point, cost-plus pricing is a widely used approach. Cost-plus pricing starts with the cost of creating and delivering a product or service and adds a fixed markup. This method is considered financially prudent—if you have calculated your costs correctly, you will never lose money on a sale. Retail outlets typically use cost-plus pricing.**

Competitive reference pricing: **With this approach, companies use the pricing of a key competitor as their primary anchor point. Depending on a company's strategy, managers will set prices at a discount below competitive pricing, at a premium above competitors, or at the same level as market pricing.**

Value-based pricing: **Pricing in this approach is based on the value customers see in a product. This method considers the price elasticity of demand and a customer's willingness to pay.**

My advice is to use all three methods in your pricing analysis, but when you make pricing decisions, lean toward value-based pricing. Cost-plus pricing is safe, but it leaves money on the table since customers may be willing to pay more than your price. Competitive reference pricing is also acceptable, but essentially you are outsourcing your pricing to the product managers of a competing company. These product managers may or may not be skilled (you can do better). This method is especially dangerous if you are the market leader.

Value-based pricing, when informed by a solid understanding of internal costs and competitive pricing, gives us the best opportunity to make healthy profits.

PROCESS OF PRICING

Let's get practical, how do you price a new product or service, or modify a price in the market today? There are eight basic steps, detailed below.

I will include an example as we move through the pricing steps. If you remember in our Day 2 discussions, we talked about the company KeepTruckin, which offers an "electronic logging device" service. An electronic logging device (ELD) tracks a commercial driver's "hours of service" with four primary categories (driving, on-duty not driving, sleeper berth, off duty). These devices ensure compliance with government regulations and more importantly, keep drowsy drivers off the road.

For this example, we will assume we are product managers for a company like KeepTruckin and need to price an electronic logging device service.

Step 1: Review your Product Strategy

A product vision, objectives, and strategy guide pricing choices. Are you trying to maximize revenue, profit, or market share? Note how your product objectives impact your pricing direction. For example, if you are striving for clear market leadership, you may need to price aggressively. Maximizing profit will lead you in a different direction.

Also, consider whether your market is elastic or inelastic. If your market is elastic, then demand rises and falls rapidly with price changes. With inelastic markets, demand stays relatively constant with price changes.

- *Electronic logging device (ELD) example:* We want to be the market leader in electronic logging devices for small and mid-sized trucking fleets. Gaining market share is our primary goal, and we will focus more on profitability after we have established market leadership. We will need to be priced below the market leaders (Omnitracs and PeopleNet) to gain initial market share, with a high value and easy-to-use product. With heavy competition and low-profit margins among trucking firms, the market for our product is price elastic.

Step 2: Understand your Costs

For this step, you'll need to work with your finance and accounting colleagues and determine the total costs (fixed and variable) of your product. You will also need to set an operating margin goal. If you were using a cost-plus pricing approach, what markup would you want to achieve? Using your total costs and the operating margin goal, you can calculate a cost-plus pricing recommendation.

- *ELD example:* Our electronic logging device service costs $10 per month per truck. Our biggest single cost is a mobile phone connection. Our operating margin target is 20% for now, but this will increase as we gain more market clout. If we use these these numbers, our cost-plus pricing recommendation is $12/month.

Step 3: Analyze your Competitors and their Pricing

Start by researching the prices of your toughest competitor. Considering your product strategy, decide if you want to price higher than this competitor, lower than this competitor, or about the same. If you are pricing higher or lower, what percentage would you target?

- *ELD example:* In the electronic logging device market in the U.S. and Canada, Omnitracs and PeopleNet are the clear market leaders. Pricing for their services is complicated, but is roughly $30/month. We think we need to price 25% below their pricing to gain market traction. From these numbers, we can calculate a "competitive reference" price recommendation of $22.50/month.

Step 4: Gauge your Value

Consider how your product benefits your customers. For example, does it streamline their workflow and save costs? If you were doing a return on investment (ROI) calculation, what "return" do customers get from your product? This benefit can be tangible (e.g., reducing expenses) or intangible (e.g., protecting a company's reputation). In the absence of direct competitors, note how high could you price before most customers would say "no thank you."

- *ELD example:* We estimate our value at $40/month. Our product is very easy to use, and government regulations mandate electronic logging devices.

Step 5: Recommend a Price

Recommend a price based on your product strategy, and the guidance from the cost-plus, competitive reference, and value-based pricing approaches (steps 2 to 4).

- *ELD example:* Our product strategy tilts us toward more aggressive pricing to gain share. The three pricing approaches give us a range: cost-plus ($12/month), competitive reference ($22.50/month) and value-based pricing ($40/month). Given our easy-to-use product, we think we can meet our growth objectives with a price of $25/month.

Step 6: Work on the Pricing Tactics

Pricing is rarely as simple as determining one price, and likely you will need to work through a host of pricing details. These include bundle pricing, channel pricing, discount guidelines for large deals, foreign currency pricing, etc.

- *ELD example:* We sell direct so we don't need to consider channel pricing, but we will need to determine pricing in many other areas: bundle pricing for our extended services (fleet tracking, tax reporting, etc.); discounts for deals with over 500 vehicles; and Canadian and U.S. currency prices.

Step 7: Gain Consensus

As product managers, we don't have unquestioned authority to set prices; we need to get organizational agreement for our proposals. You will need to review your prices with various teams and work toward alignment. This step is often concurrent with step 6. You will want to get agreement on your high-level approach, and then eventually get buy-off on details like special discounts for large deals.

- *ELD example:* We will review our top-level approach with our executive sponsors next week and are sharing details with the full sales team at our quarterly meeting.

Step 8: Experiment, Learn, and Refine

Optimal pricing takes creativity and experimentation. While some companies will do an intense round of price analysis and then park prices for two years, I don't recommend this. Given the importance of pricing on profitability, we need to continually explore, experiment, and ooch. Just as we go through discovery and delivery processes for our product, we should do the same for pricing.

- *ELD example:* Our current clients buy hardware up front and then pay a monthly subscription fee. We want to experiment whether we can expand sales with smaller fleets by charging a slightly higher subscription fee and providing the hardware for free.

DISCOUNT MANAGEMENT

If you have been in product management for any length of time, you will know that the price you *set* is not always the price you *get*. There is a difference between our official price (list price) and the price we sell at (street price). The difference is often due to discounts including marketing promotional discounts, sales channel discounts, and discounts to win large deals.

Some companies, especially those with fat profit margins, will shrug their corporate shoulders at discounts. Others, including some of the best-managed companies, will measure, track, and manage these discounts to improve profitability.

Let's assume you are selling a product with the list price of $500. You know that in the last quarter you sold 10,000 units for total revenue of

$4.25 million. Even for the mathematically challenged, the numbers don't look quite right. The average revenue per unit—dividing $4.25M by 10,000 units is $425—is well below our $500 list price. Why the difference?

The difference of $75 per unit is likely due to discounting—promotional discounts, channel discounts, big-deal discounts, lower-prices-because-we-are-nice discounts. These discounts represent a total of 15% of the list price of the product. If we were able to charge the full list price for every sale, we would have been $750,000 richer. See Figure 7.4.

List (reference) price	$500
Units sold	10,000
Revenue	$4,250,000
Average revenue per unit	$425
Discount per unit	$75
Discount percent	15%
Discount "dollars"	$750,000

Figure 7.4: Discount example

This $750,000 in discount "dollars" is an odd concept, and one that takes mental agility to grok. On the one hand, you could think that we "lost" $750,000. On the other hand, we may never have hit $4.25M in sales if we didn't discount our products—some customers simply would have never bought. Despite the strangeness of the concept, we know (and many companies know) that with tighter tracking and management, you can reduce the total discount dollars, and consequently increase your profitability.

Steps for Managing Discounts

There are three straightforward steps to managing discounts and increasing your profitability.

Quarterly discount report: **Work** with your finance team to provide a quarterly report that lists your average revenue per unit and total discounts (in amount and percentages). Ask that they prepare this report with sufficient detail for you to flex your analytical muscles. For example, you will likely want to see this data for each region, sales channel, sales district, and potentially down to individual sales reps.

Look for opportunities: **Sifting** through the data, pick two or three opportunities to reduce discount usage (and sell at a higher actual price).

You'll have to use your judgment here. When I was working for HP in Singapore as a regional product manager, our data showed that our sales in Korea were using high levels of discount, while our sales in Vietnam were much closer to our target price. Was the Korean sales team taking the easy route and habitually offering clients very low prices to get sales? Was the Vietnamese sales team exceptional in their ability to get higher prices? Neither of these was true. The Korean team was selling to very large *chaebol* companies, and these companies demanded (and received) steep discounts. The companies in Vietnam were much smaller, with far less negotiating power.

However, we also found many opportunities to curtail discounting and sell at higher prices. We found marketing promotions that were offering generous price reductions to customers who would have purchased at higher prices. We discovered that newly hired sales reps were offering low prices as a standard entry into new companies. We had channel promotions that resulted in higher wholesale inventory, but few incremental sales.

With a quarterly discount report from your finance team, look for discount-reduction opportunities. Pick out a few each quarter, and work with your marketing, sales, and channel teams to make improvements.

Provide up-front discounting guidelines: **As** you price your products, create clear discounting guidelines for your sales teams. For example, maybe you will allow sales representatives to offer up to a 5% discount for quantities below 500, 10% for deals in the 500 to 1,000 range, and up to 15% discount for very large deals over 1,000 units. See Figure 7.5.

List (reference) price	$500
1 to 500 units	Up to 5% discount
500 to 1,000 units	Up to 10% discount
More than 1,000 units	Up to 15% discount

Figure 7.5: Discount guidelines example

You can let your sales teams know that any discounting that falls within these ranges is OK, and they don't need to seek preapproval. However, if a sales representative wants to offer steeper discounts in a deal, they will need to get preapproval from a pricing committee that consists of the product manager (you), a finance representative, and a sales manager.

You don't need a PhD in pricing to manage discounts effectively. Some simple quarterly reports and up-front guidelines for your sales teams will get you a long way down the road.

LINKEDIN—PRICING EXAMPLE

Almost all of us product managers have profiles on LinkedIn, and pricing at LinkedIn provides a good example for discussion.

A basic service level at LinkedIn—with the ability for a user to create a profile, connect with others, join groups, follow companies, etc.—is free.

LinkedIn's Premium Service—priced at $59.99/month at the time of writing—allows for greater search capabilities, InMail messages, and other benefits. The $79.99/month LinkedIn Sales Navigator package helps sales professionals find and build relationships with prospects and clients. The Recruiter Lite package is $119.99/month, and the LinkedIn Recruiter Corporate tool is $999.99/month (see Figure 7.6).

Service	Price
LinkedIn Basic	Free
LinkedIn Premium Business: Get detailed business insights and expand your business	$59.99/month
LinkedIn Sales Navigator: Generate leads and build your clientele	$79.99/month
LinkedIn Recruiter Lite: Find and hire talent	$119.95/month
LinkedIn Recruiter Corporate: Support your corporate staffing workflow	$999.99/month

Source: Pricing from LinkedIn website (December 2017 and March 2018). Prices in U.S. dollars.

Figure 7.6: LinkedIn pricing

These prices are perplexing, at least initially. LinkedIn is a very valuable service, so why does the company offer the basic access for free? The services offered to premium users are not all that different than the capabilities of the basic service—there is a more tolerant set of permissions, but no dramatic new functionality. Does the premium service cost significantly more for LinkedIn, and is this the reason for the vastly different price (free vs. $59.99/month)?

The recruiter packages include a nice set of tools to help companies find and manage potential new hires, and this functionality certainly costs LinkedIn more than the basic, premium, and sales packages to maintain and enhance over time. However, these added costs can't be used to explain a $999.99/month price.

What's happening here? We can use the 3Cs of pricing—and the related pricing approaches—to understand this.

Let's start with the first C, the cost of the product. I don't have an inside view on LinkedIn's cost structure, but the company's costs are certainly above zero for the free product, and they are certainly below $59.99/month for the premium level. It's safe to say that LinkedIn is not using cost-plus pricing.

The second C, competitive environment, is also not very helpful to understand LinkedIn pricing. LinkedIn, with more than 530 million users, is really in a class by itself. For professionals, there is no other networking site with the heft of LinkedIn. If I want to find people who work at a certain company, view their background, and see if we have mutual connection—LinkedIn is the place to go. The product managers and pricing gurus at LinkedIn are not using competitive reference prices to determine their pricing.

The third C, customer value, is more helpful. If you are seeking a new job, searching for sales prospects, or combing profiles of potential hires, LinkedIn is exceptionally valuable. If the site had ten million users, it would be far less valuable, and this explains why the basic service level is free: LinkedIn recognizes that its very high number of users is precisely what creates value for job seekers, sales representatives, and corporate recruiters. A free basic service ensures that most professionals will be users.

The best explanation for differences in subscription pricing, from $59.99/month for LinkedIn Premium Business to $999.99/month for LinkedIn Recruiter Corporate, is value-based pricing. LinkedIn is valuable to premium users, but essential for recruiters. Pricing for recruiters is likely inelastic—a jump or drop in pricing may not alter demand significantly—while pricing for premium users is likely more elastic.

Bottom line: LinkedIn wraps its loving software arms around a very high number of users because it is valuable and free. This high number of users, in turn, creates exceptional benefit for a subset of users—job seekers, sales managers, recruiters. For this subset, LinkedIn is using value-based subscription pricing, and varying prices by the differential benefit each group experiences.

DAY 7 FINAL WORDS

Pricing is an area that you should say an emphatic "yes" to. Intelligent pricing is the fastest and most effective way to increase the profitability of our products, and we (and our executives) like profits.

My advice: if pricing is part of your product management job, then lean into this area. Do the hard work of pricing analysis. Understand your costs, know your competitors' pricing, and have a clear eye on the true value you bring to your customers. Consider all three pricing approaches—cost-plus, competitive reference, and value-based—but tilt toward value-based since it gives us the best opportunity for mouth-watering margins.

DAY 7 ON ONE PAGE

1. Most product managers **underinvest** in pricing, which is unfortunate. The impact of systematic pricing analysis can be enormous for a company's profitability.

2. Pricing is one of the **fastest and most effective ways** to increase the profitability of our products. Reducing fixed or variable costs are both helpful, but their impact is far below the profitability bump from effective pricing.

3. For us product managers, pricing is a **conflict-rich arena**. Sales, marketing, finance, and CEOs all have slightly different (and sometimes competing) objectives.

4. Pricing is influenced by **three Cs**. "Cost of the product" typically marks the lowest possible price since we lose money below this level. "Competitive environment" is a large factor: for most markets, customers have alternatives to our product. "Customer value" typically marks the highest possible price since there will be little (or no) demand above this point.

5. The three Cs correspond to three different pricing approaches: **cost-plus pricing, competitive reference pricing, and value-based pricing**. Value-based pricing, when informed by a solid understanding of internal costs and competitive pricing, gives us the best opportunity for attractive profits.

6. Price *setting* is not the same as price *getting*. The difference is often due to **discounts:** especially marketing promotional discounts, sales channel discounts, and discounts to win large deals. Measuring, tracking, and managing discount usage can have a strong, positive effect on profitability.

DAY 8: FINDING GROWTH

Creativity, Experimentation, and Data

From 2010 to 2014, there was incessant media hype around "MOOCs" (massive open online courses) and the potential for online education to disrupt universities and adult education. Many of the early education sites, including Coursera, Udacity, and edX, were linked to universities and offered world-class online courses, often for free.

At the same time, energetic entrepreneurs in Silicon Valley, India, the UK and elsewhere were racing to establish online course sites that offered teachers a platform to teach and earn income, and students an opportunity to learn a wide variety of skills. Founders of these new online education sites talked about democratizing learning and becoming the "eBay of education."

Edufire, CourseBridge, SuperCool School, and Udemy were all circling the same target - an online course site to serve both teachers and students. Go to the websites of most of these online platforms today, however, and you'll get redirected to Hotels.com and GoDaddy domains. Most online course sites, depressingly, didn't make it.

Udemy is the exception. Go to Udemy.com, and you'll find an overabundance of course offerings, with 15,000 new courses published in 2016 alone. More than fourteen million students have taken courses on Udemy, and this number is growing every year. The site has energy, action, and engagement, and has seen phenomenal growth since its founding in 2010.

Why is Udemy a bright star? Why have Edufire, CourseBridge and SuperCool School fallen into the internet recycling bin? Much of the answer has to do with Udemy's early and creative focus on growth.

Growth is the center point of our Day 8 discussion. Finding growth throughout the product lifecycle is a fundamental role for product managers—revenue growth, profit growth, market share growth. For startups, like Udemy in the early days, growth is an existential requirement. For long-established companies, with a full portfolio of products in the market, growth opportunities can be large (and often overlooked).

If you want to become a more strategic product manager, if you want to have more impact on your organization, finding growth is one of the areas to give a warm embrace.

In this Day 8 discussion, we'll do three things. First, we'll look at growth strategies throughout the product lifecycle, and talk through a playlist of ideas you can consider for your product. Second, we'll dive into the concept of growth hacking, which is an iterative, experimental, data-driven approach for finding rapid growth. And third, we'll circle back to the managers at Udemy, tell their story, and uncover how they found eye-opening growth.

GROWTH THROUGHOUT THE PRODUCT LIFECYCLE

If we plot market demand over time with our products, many product families follow a standard lifecycle pattern. In the early days, market demand is often very low, with a nascent and not-ready-for-prime-time product, and low awareness among potential customers. As awareness increases and the product evolves, demand starts to rise and can move through early, rapid, and late growth phases. Eventually the market demand peaks, with few new customers and flat to negative growth. At some point, the market declines and products quietly fade into obsolescence. This basic pattern is illustrated in Figure 8.1.

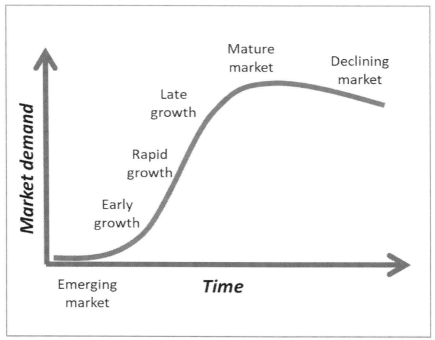

Figure 8.1: Product lifecycle

Note that not all products follow this pattern. For some new entrants, demand never materializes, and they disappear in an early morning fog. Other products may spike in fad-like fashion and then fall with equal speed. Despite the exceptions, many of the products and services we manage follow a lifecycle like the one presented here.

Our strategies for seeking growth change through the product lifecycle. In the growth phases, we typically want to play offense. We invest to grow faster than the market, and to establish a durable market leadership position. In the mature and declining stages of the market, we play defense and protect our share. See Figure 8.2.

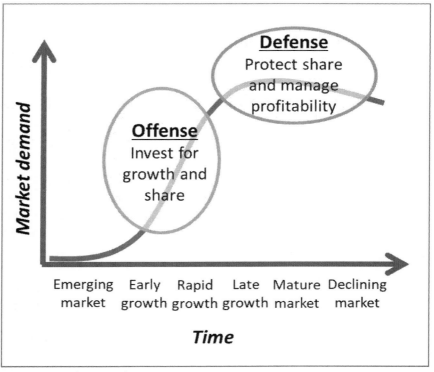

Figure 8.2: Growth strategies

Note that we find growth in both the offense and defense stages. In the offense stage, growth comes in the form of revenue and market share. In the defense phase, the focus shifts toward profit growth.

Offense

We can think about three basic approaches during the offense phase: growing our market share, growing the market, and entering new markets. Each of these approaches is detailed below.

Grow share: Here we are striving for a bigger slice of the pie. Typical actions include:

- Raising awareness through search engine optimization (SEO), content marketing (blogs, ebooks, etc.), Google AdWords, tradeshows, and other opportunities.

- Increasing trial and conversion with free trial periods, demos, samples, promotions, and sales outreach.
- Adding compelling new functionality and closing competitive feature gaps.
- Adjusting price with limited-time offers, subscription pricing, or special pricing for key customers.
- Developing new sales channels, e.g., selling online, selling through distributors, or partnering with complementary companies.
- Directly attacking competitors, for example with sales programs targeting competitive accounts.

Grow the market: Our goal here is to create a bigger pie. We can do this in many ways.

- Expanding overall market demand through viral marketing, content marketing, evangelizing at conferences, and working with key opinion leaders.
- Moving into new countries and geographies.
- Increasing revenue per customer by upselling to new services, or by identifying light or disengaged users for potential greater use of the product.
- Targeting closely related segments, for example an office chair company adding an executive chair line.
- Developing a broader ecosystem with linked applications and partnerships.
- Promoting new uses of the product by learning from innovative customers.

Enter new markets: Instead of fighting for a bigger slice of pie or creating a bigger pie, we are looking for a new pie with this approach.

- Targeting adjacent or underserved markets, either existing or new. An example might be the company Ancestry adding a health DNA service, in addition to their ancestry DNA analysis.

Defense

If we have established our market leadership position during the growth phases (by playing offense), we typically want to protect our share and enhance our profitability during the mature to declining phases. I'll spell out three, top-level approaches: protecting market share, maximizing profits, and harvesting and exiting.

Protect share: During the mature to declining phases, we want to protect our turf. We can take several actions to do this, and a partial list is below.

- Matching competitive features that are causing lost sales.
- Creating loyalty programs with incentives for renewal and repurchase.
- Enhancing purchase convenience with favorable financing terms, subscription services with automatic replenishment, etc.
- Expanding to new sales channels and optimizing current distribution.
- Offering channel sales incentives with cash for meeting targets.

Maximize profits: It might seem counterintuitive to increase profits in mature or declining markets, but many companies can do this. Since there are few new customers to be found, we can selectively reduce our marketing and sales expenses. We can focus on retaining customers instead of acquiring new customers. Retention is cheaper than acquisition, allowing us to find profit growth.

- Reducing or eliminating awareness-building for new customers (especially extensive outbound marketing like advertisements).
- Decreasing sales efforts, with a shift to less expensive customer retention.

Harvest and exit: With this approach, we manage our products for cash flow. We can raise prices and reduce our marketing expenses. As we increase prices, we will likely shed many price-sensitive customers, but we'll retain our most profitable ones. Eventually, we may decide to sell this business to another company (divest), or simply exit the market.

The offensive and defensive approaches above can be used as a playlist for your products. Start by deciding where your product sits within the product lifecycle, and then use the corresponding ideas to generate potential growth tactics. Like everything we do as product managers, you will need to experiment, measure, and course-correct as you move along. With creativity and focus, it is possible to find solid market growth even with the most stubborn products.

GROWTH HACKING

As product managers, we want to find growth for our products, regardless of whether they are new to the market or were launched ten years ago. For some of our products, a growth target of 5% per year is respectable. For other products, especially if we are part of a startup, our goal might be an astounding 20% growth per month (or more). Over the past ten to twenty years, growth hacking has emerged as a powerful approach for companies seeking this level of hyper growth.

Growth hacking is an iterative, experimental, and data-driven approach to drive rapid growth. The heritage of growth hacking is bound up with software companies, with zero to minimal marketing budgets, looking for low-cost ways of customer acquisition. For these companies, the traditional approaches to finding and acquiring new customers—especially advertising-oriented, outbound marketing—were far too expensive and never going to work.

As a quick example, think about the first time you created a profile on LinkedIn. Were you prompted by a LinkedIn-sponsored advertisement? For most of us (maybe all of us), the answer is "no." LinkedIn relied heavily on growth hacking techniques, especially viral marketing. LinkedIn gave its users the ability to import email contacts and send people a note inviting them to the service. LinkedIn would have never signed up more than 530 million users worldwide with traditional marketing and advertising.

Growth hacking is characterized by creative marketing and inventive, out-of-the-box thinking, with the goal of outrageously high growth. Decisions are data driven, with active tracking of results versus metrics. Growth hacking is an iterative approach—always curious, always evolving.

Growth hacking's toolset includes frequent experimentation, for example, AB testing of options to accelerate a customer's transition from trial to paying. We talked about ooching in Day 6 Discovery and Delivery, and growth hacking makes full use of small experiments, all in the service of customer acquisition and growth.

In many traditional companies, the line between product and marketing is fixed, and marketing teams see the product as largely immutable. With growth hacking, this distinction dissolves, and the line between product and marketing becomes porous and two way. User acquisition, onboarding, monetization, retention, and viral marketing are all built into the product itself. These areas are all prime territory for growth hacking teams to experiment and enhance.

Growth hackers also use content marketing in its various forms (blogs, how-to videos, eBooks, whitepapers, etc.). When amplified through social media and search engine optimization, content marketing (or inbound marketing) helps potential customers find us in low-cost ways. Remember all of this is in stark contrast to more traditional, and expensive, advertising-led, outbound marketing.

Small teams can drive growth best. In our Day 6 Discovery and Delivery discussion, we talked about magic in a three-person team: you, an engineering lead, and a user experience (UX) designer. If you add a data analyst and a marketing representative, you have the potential to create a stellar and impactful growth hacking team.

We talked earlier about product lifecycles. Terms like growth hacking also have a lifecycle, and the half-life on growth hacking may be far shorter than our careers as product managers. At some point, you may forget the term, but my advice is to retain and use growth hacking's best innovations: data-driven experimentation; a tight focused on growth metrics; built-in viral marketing; and a thin, porous line between product and marketing.

UDEMY

When Udemy launched in 2010, the founders and early managers had a serious problem. Why would instructors create courses for an online education site that didn't have students? And why would students come to a site that had no courses?

Udemy's managers spent six months begging instructors to create courses, setting up Skype calls with experts worldwide, pleading—with no success. Creating online courses is hard work, and the prospect of developing a new course for a likely-to-evaporate site that has no students is not appealing. The other online education startups—Edufire, CourseBridge, and SuperCool School—all faced this same vexing issue.

No instructors, no courses. No courses, no students. No students, no instructors. To break the cycle of this problem, Udemy decided to spend $3,000 and create their own course, "Raising Capital for Startups." The course itself was a success and generated $30,000 in course revenue. More important than the revenue, however, this course was used as a case study to demonstrate to reluctant instructors that Udemy could deliver the goods. If you create a course, students (and money) will come.

Udemy's initial goal was to get 100 courses on the site. To do this, Udemy's staff outlined fifteen to twenty areas that would likely have significant student interest, for example, Python coding language. They hired the company Odesk to do data mining, searching for a long list of potential instructors.

The names, email addresses, and Skype IDs of these experts were then passed on to a company in the Philippines. The starting point was a private and individualized email. Udemy used AB tests to refine these emails—500 "A" versions and 500 "B" versions—and the version that generated the most positive responses from instructors was then subjected to further AB tests.

Sometimes the results were inconclusive. If success ratios for 1,000 emails leaned 55% "A" and 45% "B," did this matter? Udemy's managers used a combination of hard data and human judgment to make decisions and improve the effectiveness of their outreach.

With this outreach, Udemy ran into a second problem. Instructors would say "yes," but never finish the course. Udemy's answer was to recontact these instructors and let them know that Udemy was planning to run a promotion on their course in three to four weeks. Could the instructors have their courses ready by then? This tactic not only increased the speed of course creation, but it also increased the overall completion rates. In other words, an artificial deadline pushed instructors to finish, and finish in a hurry.

With the first set of courses now on the site, Udemy began a program of partnerships with technology-oriented email newsletters. They approached newsletters, like Startup Digest, and asked for visibility for Udemy's courses in exchange for 50% revenue sharing. The managers at Udemy were serious and thorough in their work and began reaching three to four million potential students per month.

Not all Udemy's marketing tactics were successful. They found that if they were spending $50,000/month on Google and Facebook ads, they could turn this up or down the following month, with little impact on the number of incoming students. The growth Udemy was experiencing during this time was mostly organic, and very little was coming from paid acquisition.

As cofounder, Gagan Biyani, recounts Udemy's early history, he describes a culture focused on rapid-fire AB tests, but also one that stopped talking to students and teachers, one that overlooked the more qualitative factors driving the business. Udemy was studying the averages, not the anecdotes, and the next stage of growth was largely driven by correcting this.

Udemy refocused on instructor and user experience in the following years, working to create a site with high loyalty. I recently refreshed my own Udemy course and found the instructor tools and video guidance exceptionally useful.

Today Udemy has over seventeen million users and 55,000 courses. The courses span sixty different languages. Despite the short time period, Udemy is a far different company than it was in 2010 when it was begging experts to create courses.

Takeaways

For us product managers working to generate growth, I'll highlight a few key takeaways from Udemy's experience:

1. Udemy had an **intense and persistent growth focus**. Udemy didn't just reach out to some instructors asking them to create courses, they emailed thousands per week. The company didn't just partner with some technology newsletters, they partnered with nearly every technology newsletter, reaching three to four million people per month.

2. **Creativity, experimentation, and openness** drove Udemy's learning and success. Emails to potential instructors were refined with AB tests, and refined again, and again. Instructors not finishing their courses? Let's try an arbitrary deadline and see if it works. Udemy's founders and managers recognized they didn't know the answers, but needed to discover the answers.

3. Udemy balanced the **quantitative and qualitative.** Initially, Udemy focused heavily on AB tests and other quantitative methods, but eventually realized they needed to reach out directly to instructors and students, hear their stories, and create an experience that was loved and not just liked.

FINDING GROWTH: STEP BY STEP

Let's get very practical. If you are going to find growth for your product, how do you do it?

1. Start with your **product strategy**. Review your product vision, objectives, and strategy that we discussed on Day 4. We want to grow, but we want to grow in the right direction to set up our products for long-term success. Strategy gives us that direction.

2. Gather a **growth team**. Prime candidates include an engineering lead, a UX/UI designer, a marketing representative, and a data analyst.

3. Decide where you are at in the **product lifecycle**. Are you in the early and energetic growth phases or in a mature and declining market? Do you want to play offense or defense?

4. Consider a **broad spectrum of growth ideas**. In our earlier discussion, I included the "offense" and "defense" playlists for finding growth. Use these as thought starters, and brainstorm ideas for your product.

5. **Prioritize your ideas** and decide which to pursue in the next three months. Make your choices based on strategic fit, ease of implementation, and potential payoff. If you can, add a growth objective and key metrics to the OKRs we discussed on Day 5.

6. **Experiment, learn, and refine**. Try out your ideas and track success (or the lack of it). Don't assume you have the answers; assume that you need to discover the answers through a series of small experiments. Be open, keep learning, and—like the managers at Udemy—be persistent.

DAY 8 FINAL WORDS

Finding revenue, profit, and share growth is one of our central jobs as product managers. If you are a product manager for a startup, growth is your lifeblood and will keep you out of economic recycling bins. If you are working at a larger corporation, there is a good chance you have solid growth opportunities, even from seemingly stale products.

My advice is to consider growth one your prime jobs, and one with a smile-inducing upside. Gather a team, explore your options, experiment, refine, and experiment again. Stay focused, be persistent, and watch your numbers rise.

DAY 8 ON ONE PAGE

1. Finding **revenue, profit, and share growth** is a fundamental role of product managers. Many long-established products have strong, but often overlooked, growth potential.

2. Our strategies for seeking growth vary through the **product lifecycle**. In the growth phases, we typically want to play offense, with a focus on revenue and share growth. In the more mature phases, we want to play defense, protecting our share and increasing our profits.

3. In the **growth stages** of a product—when we play offense—we can grow our share, grow the market, or enter new and adjacent markets.

4. When market growth is **flat or declining**, we can often increase our profitability by shifting from customer acquisition to customer retention. At some point, "harvest and exit" may be the most appropriate strategy.

5. **Growth hacking** is an iterative, experimental, and data-driven approach to drive rapid customer acquisition. Many growth hacking approaches were developed at software startups, with little or no money for traditional, outbound marketing.

6. The managers at the online course site, **Udemy**, have had an intense, persistent, and successful focus on growth over the past years. Udemy's managers had creative ideas about what would bring new instructors and students to their site, and they used frequent experimentation and metrics tracking to refine these ideas.

DAY 9: EXCELLENCE IN PRODUCT MANAGEMENT

Hungry, Humble, and Disciplined

On our best days, we—as product managers—are hungry, humble, and disciplined. We are passionate about customer success and aggressively seek growth. We have the self-confidence to appreciate our own ideas, but the self-awareness to know what we can't know. We actively cultivate a diversity of ideas from others, through openness and respect. We learn by experimentation, we ooch. We are goal-oriented, long-range thinkers who simultaneously drive near-term action. We get runs on the board. We practice and perfect our craft. We care deeply about our products, our teams, our customers. On our best days, this is who we are.

Over the past eight lessons, we have discussed the importance of finding a better balance between the strategic and tactical. We have looked at specific areas of focus: customer analysis, competitive analysis, strategy development, prioritization, discovery and delivery development, pricing, and finding growth. Individually none of these areas will make you a strategic product manager, but collectively they can amplify your impact— to the benefit of your customers and your company.

In our Day 9 discussion, let's pull these elements together and talk about the recipe for becoming more strategic. I'll assume that you, as a product manager, are either stepping into a new role or are ready to re-energize your current role. This recipe will specify actions over three quarters (nine months), looking for both early wins and long-range impact. Like all good recipes, you'll need to adapt this to your own kitchen and your own ingredients.

If this recipe represents your top-level, go-forward action plan, then we also need to talk about two underlying areas to help you find excellence: your attitude and approach, and your support network. We'll dive into both areas toward the end of our discussion.

THE THREE-QUARTER PLAN

If you are stepping into a new product management role (or rejuvenating your current role) you will want to quickly establish your credibility, energize your team, and bump up support from your management. For this, we need quick, visible success. "Early wins" is the theme of your first three months.

Securing a path toward long-term wins is your challenge in the second quarter, months four through six. During this quarter, we need to dive into the vision, objectives, and strategy of your product. We also need to craft a path for revenue, profit, and share growth. Both efforts take time and work, grounded in market, customer, and competitive intelligence. "Strategy and growth" is the theme of your second quarter.

Strong product managers, with a motivated and skilled team, can have a large impact in six months. This impact can be fresh and fragile, however, and needs experimentation, learning, and evolution. The goal is to steer your product toward multi-year customer delight, competitive advantage, and generous profitability. "Refinement" is the theme of your third quarter.

Let's step through each of these quarters. You can refer to the Figures 9.1, 9.2, and 9.3 to keep this recipe organized in your mind.

Q1: Early Wins

Our recipe starts with customers, as it should. As quickly as possible, preferably within two or three weeks, get out of the office and interview your customers (and your competitors' customers and non-users).

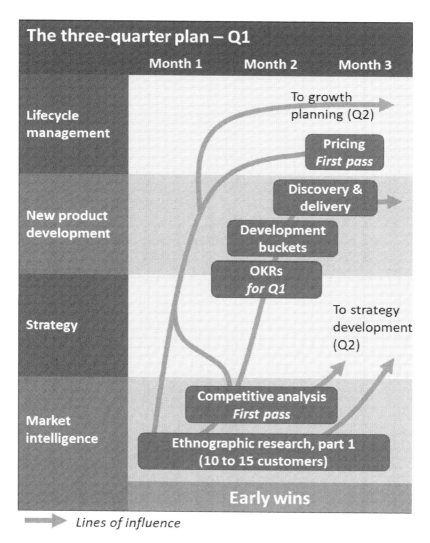

Figure 9.1: The three-quarter plan (Q1)

There are multiple reasons for doing ethnographic research very early in your work. Without a solid understanding of your customers, you will have little to contribute in your product planning meetings. Repeating what you heard from a sales rep or a channel partner, or just repeating the corporate consensus around your customers, is a quick way to make your voice irrelevant. Developing a deep and empathetic understanding of your customers gives you a unique perspective. It gives you credibility.

My advice is to start early with ethnographic research. Over the first three months, you should have at least ten to fifteen in-depth interviews with customers.

The next step of our recipe is to do a quick, first-pass competitive analysis. Don't spend too much time here, just get the basics on your direct competitors and any looming disruptive technologies. As we discussed in Day 3, competitive analysis is hugely important, but let's wait for our second quarter to do in-depth analysis.

The third step, likely at the beginning of month two, is to craft two or three OKRs (objectives and key results) to guide your development efforts. Your product team may have limited experience working with quarterly OKRs, so you may need to evangelize the concept. Highlight the simplicity of the approach; OKRs will help you focus your development efforts on a tiny handful of changes that will have a strong market impact.

At this point, you may not have a deep understanding of your product's long-term strategy to guide these OKRs. In my experience product teams often know a few of their next important steps and can guide you. Your managers will also have their hot-button items. Look for low-hanging fruit that the organization values.

As a fourth step, together with your engineering leads, craft your development buckets. Be sure to include target percentages for each category. As you'll remember from our Day 5 discussion, development buckets help you and your team focus efforts on your OKRs. They provide discipline to say "no" to extraneous distractions.

With OKRs and development buckets in place, step five is to initiate a discovery and delivery process. If it makes sense for your product, create a three-person team: your engineering lead, your user experience (UX/UI) person, and yourself. If your team is new to this process, pick an area integral to your OKRs, sketch early prototypes, and include these into your ethnographic interviews. Listen, learn, and refine.

Your last task in Q1 is to analyze product pricing—at a first-pass, draft level. The intent is to get familiar with the issues and opportunities around pricing. This investigation will inform your strategy and growth planning in Q2.

Early wins and positive momentum are essential for your first three months. Michael Watkins, in his book *The First 90 Days*, writes about this concept. The book is targeted at executives moving into a new role, but much of the wisdom and advice is relevant for us product managers. In the first three months, Watkins explains that it is critical to do several things simultaneously: learn, build credibility, and generate early wins that the company values.

Watkins highlights the goal of creating virtuous cycles (as opposed to vicious cycles). The virtuous cycle during our first three months goes something like this:

1. **Ethnographic research** gives you (and your team) greater customer understanding and helps guide your choice of OKRs.
2. **OKRs** and **development buckets** focus your product team's efforts on a few promising opportunities. Distractions are swept aside.
3. Your development team, with its newfound focus, delivers **key enhancements**.
4. Key product enhancements increase **management confidence** that you and your team can deliver results. They give you support for farther-reaching product changes.

This virtuous cycle should be energizing for you and your team. Enjoy the tailwinds as you move into Q2.

Q2: Strategy and Growth

During Q2, you will want to continue with ethnographic research. As you prepare for deeper strategy and growth analysis, you will uncover new and intriguing questions to ask. You should also do this in Q3 (and Q4 and beyond); this research never stops.

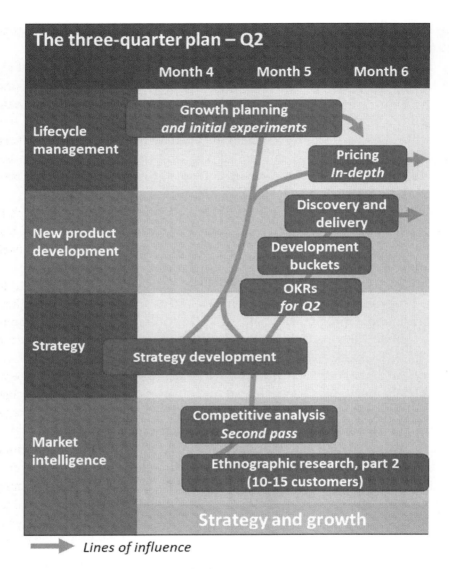

Figure 9.2: The three-quarter plan (Q2)

In Q1, we surveyed the competitive landscape. We should re-engage in Q2, at greater depth. Go ahead and do the full scope of competitive analysis as described in Day 3. A full competitive review feeds into your strategy project, and informs growth planning and pricing.

At the heart of our Q2 work are two interrelated projects: strategy development and growth planning. Start with strategy. At the end of month three (or the beginning of month four), you should pull together a team and create a vision, objectives, and strategy for your product. If you remember from our Day 4 discussion, developing a strategy takes analysis, thinking, debating, prodding, and pulling. All this takes time. If you are stepping into a new role, taking on a strategy project in your first three months might cause indigestion.

On the other hand, you don't want to wait too long. Strategy work is vital to much of what we do as product managers. If we want to go big, if we want customers to drool over our products, if we want to knock back our competitors, we need a strategy. Q2 is the right time to dive in.

When your strategy work begins to gel, you should use the results to guide your next set of quarterly OKRs and development buckets. In our first set of OKRs (in Q1), we picked two or three areas that your engineers and management team agreed would have a solid impact. Your second set of OKRs should be guided by a product strategy.

Remember that we want to set up our products and teams for long-term success. One of our best tools for customer delight, competitive advantage, and crisp profits is a development team focused on delivering to a strategy. Don't pass up this tool.

With a new set of OKRs and updated development buckets, continue with your discovery and delivery process. Use your learnings in Q1 to refine your approach. Maybe 3D models are giving you the most intriguing feedback, if so, keep doing this. Maybe simple explanations of product ideas are yielding insights, while detailed schematics are confusing your customers. Discovery and delivery is all about experimentation and learning; it's all about ooching. Ooch with your process as well, finding ways to interact with the customers that give you the best and most accurate guidance.

Growth planning, as described in Day 8, is your next step. Use the output of your strategy work to help guide this. Remember we don't want to grow in any direction, we want to grow toward market opportunities that we can uniquely fill.

Growth planning also informs our pricing work. We did first pass pricing work in Q1. Toward the end of Q2, re-engage with pricing at greater depth. As we discussed in Day 7, pricing is one of the top areas we, as product managers, can impact our companies. Higher profits will make your managers smile, generating confidence and support.

Q3: Refinement

If you have successfully followed this recipe, by month seven you will have demonstrated early wins, you will have a strategy in place, and you will be experimenting with growth and pricing opportunities. If you step away now, the team will be in better shape—in fact significantly better shape—than when you walked in the door, but long-term product success is still fragile. We live within competitive markets and stubborn corporate cultures. We still need to build momentum.

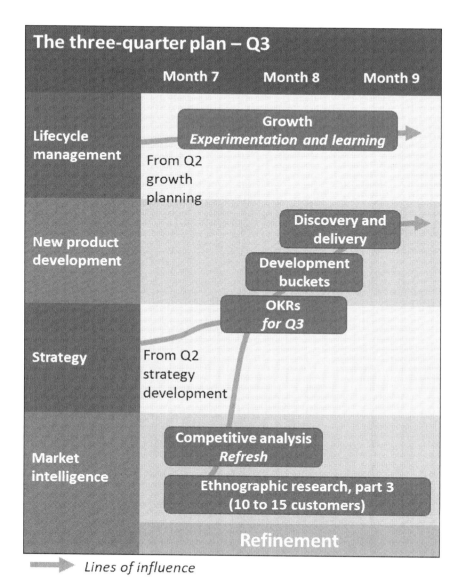

Figure 9.3: The three-quarter plan (Q3)

Q3 is a time to refine, strengthen, and solidify your direction. Continue with ethnographic research, refresh your competitive analysis, and use your strategy to guide Q3 OKRs and development buckets. Test product prototypes with your customers. Learn, evolve, and test again. Release enhancements when you have confidence in their market fit. Find new paths toward growth, letting your data and strategy guide you. Build virtuous cycles, enjoy newfound management support, relish your market share gains, and grin when customers gush over your product.

APPROACH AND ATTITUDE

The three-quarter recipe I outlined above (and detailed throughout this book) should be your action plan going forward. Underlying this action plan—and critical to becoming a more strategic product manager—are your approach and attitude. Excellent product managers are hungry, humble, and disciplined. Let's talk through each of these.

Characteristics of excellent product managers	
Hungry	Passionate about customer success
	Aggressively focused on growth
	Intensely curious
	Manage ourselves for high energy
Humble	Focused on customer, team, and company success
	Intellectually modest
	Respectful of our colleagues and teammates
Disciplined	Goal-oriented, long-range thinkers
	Committed and persistent
	Know our products
	Practice and hone our craft

Figure 9.4: Characteristics of excellent product managers

Hungry

Being hungry is all about the energy we bring to our work—the passion we have for improving the lives of our customers, the aggressiveness with which we pursue growth opportunities, and the insane curiosity we have for all areas surrounding our products, markets, and customers.

Beyond our fundamental motivation and drive, we also need to actively manage our own energy—with rhythmic cycles of intense work punctuated by rest and rejuvenation.

Passionate about customer success: One of our primary motivators as product managers is the desire to improve the lives of our customers. We need to empathize with them, feel their problems, see their opportunities, and be passionate about their success. How can we do this?

Ethnographic research is probably our strongest tool here. We need to get out, talk to people, hear their challenges, and absorb their energy and passion. Note the "get out" part—you can't do this by having a few, scattered meetings with your sales team. Our friends at Pragmatic Marketing use the acronym "NIHITO" —nothing important happens in the office.

Aggressively focused on growth: If you are at a startup funded by venture capital, the need for growth will sit on every molecule of office air. However, if you are at a long-established company managing mature products, you may be tempted to drift, you may be tempted to babysit. Finding growth, as we noted in our Day 8 discussion, is one of our fundamental roles as product managers. If you are working in a slow-moving product space, with a complacent team, how can you fuel the fire to drive growth?

My suggestion is to develop strong growth plans, as outlined in Day 8, with experimentation and creativity. From my experience, the act of developing these plans - and tapping into your team's best ideas - adds energy and motivation to even the most jaded product group. Early wins, even small successes, will add further motivation, setting the stage for even bigger wins and bigger growth.

Intensely curious: As excellent product managers, we are curiosity outliers; we want to know market trends, government regulations, customer problems and opportunities, product usage data, and every time a competitor's CEO talks about strategy on a podcast.

Learning takes time, however. You'll need to build free space into your schedule to wander (literally and figuratively) through your market space, letting your curiosity explore and follow leads. Ethnographic research will open new vistas and opportunities. Industry analysts, trade conferences, and academic research can spark ideas and new perspectives. NIHITO applies here as well—office walls can dull your curiosity. Much better to get out, explore, and learn.

Manage ourselves for high energy: Our jobs as product managers have heavy demands and we are tempted to work long hours every day. Our success, however, is typically not determined by the time we spend, but rather by the energy we invest in the time that we spend. Jim Loehr and Tony Schwartz talk about this concept in their book *The Power of Full Engagement.* "Energy, not time, is the fundamental currency of high performance," they write.

In our journey from tactical to strategic, managing ourselves for high energy takes on special importance. For product managers who are primarily tactical, longer hours can lead to higher productivity. For strategic work, long hours, exhaustion, and lack of sleep are counterproductive. For the Day 2 through Day 8 strategic areas articulated in this book, you need thought and analysis, you need fresh and creative thinking, and you need energy.

A few nights ago, I watched the closing ceremony of the Olympics. It helps to think of ourselves as Olympic athletes: at times our jobs are every bit as demanding as speed skating or 4x100 m relays, and we do them every day, not once in four years. Like Olympic athletes, we need to eat well, work intensely, take frequent rest breaks, be physically active, and sleep. It's only by doing this that we'll have the day-to-day energy to find insight and excellence.

Humble

I worked for a San Diego-based company that actively recruited and rewarded humble employees. At first glance, "humble" is an odd characteristic for an aggressively growing company to seek in its workers. Why humble? Technology companies, especially those in the U.S., are not known for their humility.

And yet, I see this characteristic in some of the best product managers I've worked with. These product managers are dedicated to customer and team success. They are far less focused on self-promotion. They actively listen to ideas from a diverse set of people, never letting their pride get in the way of learning. They don't talk about their "personal brand." They have deep respect and gratitude for their team members from engineering, finance, client services, marketing, and sales.

Focused on customer, team, and company: David Brooks, in his book *The Road to Character*, writes about a culture that he calls "the Big Me" which has crept up on us over the past seventy years. This culture encourages people to see themselves at the center of the universe, to see themselves as extraordinary, to feel that someone should write their biography. If you want to be a strategic and effective product manager, I wouldn't recommend this.

On our best days as product managers, we are focused on customer, team, and company success (in that order). Any personal success is a by-product of a relentless focus on the success of others. At the end of the day, it is not about us, but about the value we bring to our customers, our team, and our companies. In the most courageous product managers, this is what I see.

Intellectually modest: In *Thinking, Fast and Slow*, Daniel Kahneman notes that as humans, we have an "almost unlimited ability to ignore our ignorance." As product managers, this can get us into deep trouble.

Excellent product managers view their own market knowledge with modesty and humility. We think we know what products and features will succeed in the market, but we put our assumptions to the test. We experiment, we share prototypes, we release in small increments. We assume we are wrong (and we often are). We are open to ideas and wisdom from a diverse set of sources: our engineers, our UX/UI designers, our competitors, our customers. We aren't true believers in any one approach, but instead, lean toward the experimental and empirical.

I find this approach liberating. As product managers, we don't need to *know* the answers, we just need to *find* the answers.

Respectful of our colleagues and teammates: One of our core tasks as product managers is to make our products, and product teams, successful. We typically don't have organizational authority over our teams; our engineers and UX/UI designers don't report to us. We need to work with them in a collaborative, respectful fashion. Arrogance won't get you very far as a product manager.

A key success factor, especially in your first three months, is to lay the groundwork for strong teamwork—creating supportive alliances with the members of your extended product team. Start by assuming good intent. All of us on a product team want to excite customers and spook competitors, we all want market success. Build alliances by supporting your colleagues, being persistent, being dependable, making plans, and following through.

Also note that as we move from tactical product management to becoming more strategic, we need to evolve our people and team skills. For very tactical product managers, technical knowledge might be enough. However, as we become more strategic, soft skills take on new importance.

We need to expand our repertoire to include cultural and political elements: how to get things done, how to build cohesive teams, how to manage conflict, how to maintain supportive relationships. If you move into people management and eventually become an executive, these skills just get more important (consider product management as great training for future promotions).

Disciplined

A third characteristic of the best product managers on this planet is discipline. We are goal-oriented, long-range thinkers. We are committed, persistent, and diligent. We know our products as users and as technologists. And, importantly, we practice and hone our craft as product managers. We get better every day.

Goal-oriented, long-range thinkers: I'm often surprised at how many business people lack a longer-range perspective, with a steady focus on the next three to six months, and blinders after that. Our jobs as product managers force us to break out of this habit. If the product managers at a competing company have an exclusively near-term focus, then rejoice. You'll swamp them in one to three years.

Strategic planning, OKRs, development buckets—the approaches outlined in this book will help you make long-range, strategic thinking a habitual part of your standard processes.

Committed and persistent: In a 2009 study, "Which CEO characteristics and abilities matter?" the authors found that the traits most correlated with success include attention to detail, persistence, efficiency, and analytical thoroughness. All of these are characteristics of successful product managers as well.

It is not a coincidence that the first product managers in technology companies are typically CEOs and founders. The broad management skills we learn as product managers are the same skills that help make CEOs successful. Commitment, persistence, and thoroughness are high on the list.

Know our products: In the Day 2 portion of the book, we discussed the Kano model and how customers have basic, performance, and attractive needs. For product managers, knowing our products is a basic need, it is a must-be requirement.

You should actively use your product or closely work with people who are using it. You should tear it apart, dissect its components, and explore all the hidden nooks. You should understand the core technology, features, benefits, strengths, and weaknesses. For a comparison set, use competing products.

We want to be credible in front of a wide range of people, including engineers, marketing, sales, support staff, partners, and customers. To do this well, we need to know our products.

Practice and hone our craft: To become an excellent product manager, we need to practice.

Quoting David Brooks again, this time from *The Social Animal*, "The key factor separating geniuses from the merely accomplished is the ability to get better and better gradually over time." Much of what we do as product managers melds well with this. The discovery and delivery approach detailed in Day 6 is less about divine inspiration and more about stepwise improvement.

We should use the same approach for our own craft of product management; we should deliberately practice, experiment, ooch. We need to be self-critical and fully understand which parts of our work are succeeding and which parts lack spark.

As one example, getting a depth of information from ethnographic research takes skill. I've probably conducted over 500 interviews in my career, with many more to come. After every interview, I ask myself how I could have done the interview better. Did I inadvertently ask a leading question? Did I actively listen for subtle areas of disagreement to avoid my own confirmation bias? Did I observe the environment and pick up on non-verbal clues? How can I improve next time?

Applying this type of disciplined practice to critical areas of our work is one of the keys to excellence. Our goal is to get better every day.

SUPPORT NETWORK

To become a more strategic product manager, you will need to gather a diverse advice-and-counsel network. I'll suggest four different categories of advisers:

Technical: Engineers, scientists and other experts can help you understand the defining technical aspects of your product. Seek out a small set of people with insight and patience.

Cultural/political: As product managers we work in and among a wide range of groups: engineering, marketing, sales, client services, finance, and executive management. The skills needed to be effective at this can be overwhelming. We need to create a shared vision, nurture support for our initiatives, develop alliances, and get to "yes." A cultural and political adviser can help us navigate these corporate mazes.

Strategic: Systematic, longer-term, strategic thinkers are rare in most companies. As you develop a strategy for your product, search for someone with these skills, and include them in your informal support network, or more formally as part of your strategy team.

Product management: As product managers, we work in both a vertical industry (our company and market segment) and a horizontal function (product management). We can sometimes feel isolated in our vertical industry, confined to our company's product team, narrowly focused on our internal problems and debates.

Using your advice-and-counsel network, it is important to step outside of this. Tap into product management blogs, go to local meetups, and join ProductCamps or other events. A product management coach can also help you adapt this book's nine-month plan to your specific situation.

DAY 9 FINAL WORDS

The goal of this book is to help you become a more strategic product manager: to create powerful product portfolios, delight your customers, punch your competitors, and earn mouth-watering profits.

To become more strategic—to go big—we need to say a gentle "no" to the non-core tactical elements of our jobs, and to say an emphatic "yes" to all those elements that have a long-range impact. We need to say "yes" to ethnographic research, strategy development, discovery and delivery, and a creative search for growth. We need to say "yes" to curiosity, experimentation, and learning. We need to say "yes" to a persistent and energetic drive toward excellence.

Product managers stepping into a new role (or re-energizing their current role) can have a strong impact on their companies and their products in three to nine months. As product managers, we are gifted—more so than other roles in our companies—with influential positions. We aren't wall decorations. We steal market share from our competitors, month by month. We innovate, refine, and evolve our products. We set up our products and teams for long-term success. We focus and deliver.

I hope all your product management work goes exceptionally well. Step forward, find a better balance between the tactical and strategic, and go big.

DAY 9 ON ONE PAGE

1. Product managers can have a significant, long-term impact on their products and product teams in **three quarters** (nine months).

2. **"Early wins"** are the focus of the first quarter. Early wins help generate credibility, positive momentum, and management support.

3. **Strategy development** and **growth planning** both happen in the second quarter. These in turn guide OKRs, development buckets, and pricing.

4. After six months, progress will be both tangible and fragile. Q3 is a time to **refine, strengthen, and solidify** a product direction, pointing toward long-term success.

5. Many excellent product managers show a common set of characteristics—they tend to be **hungry, humble, and disciplined**.

6. Developing a strong **advice-and-counsel network** becomes more important as product managers become more strategic. Seek technical, political/cultural, and strategic advisers. Also link to the field of product management—experts, events, and best practices.

QUIZ

Test Your Knowledge

QUESTIONS

Question 1: Ethnographic research, when done well, centers around:
a)   Internet surveys
b)   Fifteen-minute phone interviews
c)   Interviews with customers in one of your office conference rooms
d)   A combination of interviews and observation, at the place where the customer uses your product (or our competitors' products)

Question 2: Hotels spend a lot of money to ensure that hot water is available soon after guests turn on the shower. Having quick access to hot water is what kind of need in the Kano model?
a)   Attractive need (delighter)
b)   Performance need
c)   Basic need
d)   It's not a need (cold showers are invigorating)

Question 3: Sales representatives can sometimes cause issues during ethnographic research. What are some of the ways to manage this?

a) Explain that you want unfiltered user feedback, and the best way to do this is to let users express themselves without introducing bias
b) Ask sales reps to hold their questions and comments until the end of the interview
c) Do the interviews without sales reps
d) All of the above

Question 4: Why do market-leading companies sometimes get overtaken by disruptive technologies?
a) Management denial
b) Resistance to change
c) High profitability
d) All of the above

Question 5: Why should you monitor competitors?
a) Anticipate market changes
b) Spot new product enhancement ideas
c) Optimize your pricing
d) All of the above

Question 6: Desktop laser printers are a category that has been hit with disruptive technology over the past fifteen years, with fewer pages printed. What do you think is the disruptive technology?
a) Inkjet printing
b) Smartphones, tablets, and laptops
c) New Helvetica fonts
d) Ultra-low-cost competitors

Question 7: Which one of the following is *not* true?
a) Strategy development is best done alone since it takes deep analysis
b) Good strategy development identifies competitive differentiators, now and in the future
c) Strategy development spells out your economic logic (i.e., how you will make money)

d) Strategy development is one of the most challenging things we do as product managers

Question 8: A product vision should be:
a) Compelling
b) Ambitious
c) Motivating
d) All of the above

Question 9: Which of the following is true about vision and strategy?

a) A strategy should be in place for three to five years, with very little change, to allow for product development teams to complete long-range projects
b) A product vision should remain reasonably stable over time, providing a "true north" for product development teams
c) As product managers, we should change our strategy as quickly as our development teams can respond

Question 10: "OKR" stands for:
a) Objectives and key results
b) Obstacles keep receding
c) Observation and key response
d) Other known redundancies

Question11: Which of the following is true about OKRs?
a) Hitting a score of 1.0 (i.e., 100% goal achievement) is ideal
b) You should spell out the "how" (i.e., how you will solve an issue or meet your goal)
c) Teams should feel empowered with a well-managed OKR process; they have a goal with concrete measurements, and they are tasked with figuring out how to achieve this
d) Within Google, OKRs are kept private—one team does not see another team's OKRs

Question 12: Which of the following is true about roadmaps?

a) Roadmaps can be an effective way of showing a product's evolution over time
b) Roadmaps can sometimes cause issues when sales teams communicate them prematurely to clients, who then come to expect delivery of roadmap items
c) Many of the product management software tools (like Aha! and ProductPlan) offer the capability to create product roadmaps
d) All of the above

Question 13: If an executive comes by your desk with her favorite product enhancement idea, and requests that it be developed, one of the best responses is:
a) Yes
b) No
c) Our roadmap is full, and we have no bandwidth for this
d) It's a good idea. We'll run it through our discovery and delivery process, and test market reaction

Question 14: The discovery portion of "discovery and delivery" usually does not include:
a) Prototypes
b) Experimentation
c) Final, fully developed products
d) Testing for market fit

Question 15: For many companies, the ideal team to lead a discovery and delivery process consists of:
a) Product manager, user experience designer (UX), engineering lead
b) Product manager, marketing communications lead, sales representative
c) Engineering lead, quality assurance representative, technical support
d) Product manager, client services manager, finance representative

Question 16: Most product managers:

a) Spend too much time on pricing
b) Spend too little time on pricing
c) Have PhDs in pricing

Question 17: Which has a greater impact on a company's profitability?
a) 1% increase in price
b) 1% improvement in fixed costs
c) 1% improvement in variable costs

Question 18: One of the best ways to manage pricing for large enterprise deals, is to:
a) Empower sales teams to offer discounted prices down to a certain level, but ask them to get approval from a pricing committee before pricing below this
b) Ask sales teams get approval from you before offering any discounted price to enterprise clients
c) Allow sales teams to sell at whatever price is needed to get the deal
d) Refuse any discounted pricing, instead sticking with your original list price

Question 19: Which is *not* true about growth hacking?
a) Growth hacking incorporates growth components into the product itself (e.g., on-boarding tools, viral marketing, etc.)
b) Udemy used growth hacking tactics
c) Growth hacking strives for a steady and respectable 5% revenue growth per year
d) Growth hacking's heritage is with startup companies (like LinkedIn and Facebook) that wanted rapid increases in the number of their users

Question 20: In mature and declining markets:
a) One way to maximize profit is to reduce the price to gain market share
b) A company should invest heavily in new finding new customers, (e.g., with new ad campaigns)

c) Companies may consider a "harvest and exit" strategy, by raising prices and reducing market investments

Question 21: In markets with rapid growth, good approaches include:
a) Using viral marketing tactics
b) Reaching out to new, untapped customer segments
c) Expanding into new geographies
d) All of the above

ANSWERS

Answer 1: D

On-site interviews and observations are the best way to discover the articulated and unarticulated needs of your customers, and tease out underlying motivations. (Day 2)

Answer 2: C

If hot water is available quickly, hotel guests step into the shower, but they aren't thrilled and don't jump for joy. Hot water is simply an expectation (unless you are at a cheap backpacker hostel). (Day 2)

Answer 3: D

We love sales reps, but need to manage them when we are doing ethnographic research. (Day2)

Answer 4: D

Denial, resistance to change, and high profitability all blind companies to the threat of disruptive technology. (Day 3)

Answer 5: D

We monitor competitors for all these reasons. (Day 3)

Answer 6: B

Smartphones, tablets, and laptops provide information in a flexible, updated, and mobile way, causing steep drops in pages printed. (Day 3)

Answer 7: A

Strategy work is best done in a cross-functional team. It requires deep thinking, discussion, and a diversity of perspectives. (Day 4)

Answer 8: D

The best product visions are compelling, ambitious, and motivating. They speak to the "why" and are less about the "how." (Day 4)

Answer 9: B

A strategy should be reasonably stable—not changing every three months—but we also need to iterate and enhance our strategy as the market changes and new opportunities arise. A product vision should paint a long-term direction. (Day 4)

Answer 10: A

Objectives and key results. (Day 5)

Answer 11: C

An OKR process, managed correctly, empowers teams to be creative and move quickly. Consistently hitting a score of 1.0 suggests you are too conservative in setting your OKRs. The "how" is best determined when the teams begin investigation and development (i.e., through discovery and delivery). Google's OKR process is open and transparent, in fact, they see this as a key aspect of the process. (Day 5)

Answer 12: D

All of these statements about roadmaps are true. (Day 5)

Answer 13: D

Your executive's idea might be good or bad, but we can easily test this with customers. (Day 6)

Answer 14: **C**

Usually, we are testing product concepts that have not yet been developed. (Day 6)

Answer 15: **A**

There is magic in the combination of a product manager, user experience designer (UX), and engineering lead. The diversity of perspectives is especially helpful. (Day 6)

Answer 16: **B**

Typically, product managers underinvest in pricing relative to its importance for their organizations. (Day 7)

Answer 17: **A**

A 1% improvement in price can have a significant impact on a company's profitability. (Day 7)

Answer 18: **A**

Empowering sales teams to offer discounts to a certain level, but requiring permission beyond this, is a very effective process. Asking sales representatives to get preapproval on all deal discounts is tedious and overly bureaucratic. On the other hand, giving sales reps full freedom can cause an unnecessary drop in profitability. Refusing all enterprise deal discounts will cause you to lose profitable deals to competitors. (Day 7)

Answer 19: **C**

Growth hacking targets are typically much more aggressive. Some startup companies look to grow their user base by 20% per month (or more). (Day 8)

Answer 20: **C**

"Harvest and exit" may be a good strategy to maximize profits at the tail-end of a product's lifecycle. Reducing prices is likely a losing strategy since you will need to gain significant market share to offset the lower per-unit profit. Typically, there are very few new customers to be found in declining markets, so new ad campaigns make little sense. (Day 8)

Answer 21: D

All these approaches are worth considering during the growth phases of a product lifecycle. (Day 8)

REFERENCES

Alberta Agriculture and Forestry, Food and Value Added Processing Division, and Rural Development Branch. "Methods to Price Your Products." *Alberta Agriculture and Forestry*, 13 Oct. 2017, http://www1.agric.gov.ab.ca/$department/deptdocs.nsf/all/agdex1133

Ancestry. "We're a Science and Technology Company with a Very Human Mission." *Our Story | Ancestry Corporate*, 2018, www.ancestry.com/corporate/about-ancestry/our-story

Anders, George. "LinkedIn Reprices Premium Services, Hoping Users Won't Turn Furious." *Forbes*, Forbes Magazine, 26 Sept. 2016, www.forbes.com/sites/georgeanders/2015/01/06/linkedin-reprices-premium-services-hoping-users-wont-turn-furious/#6bbe84a1ffdc

Anderson, James C., et al. "Why the Highest Price Isn't the Best Price." *MIT Sloan Management Review*, 2010, https://sloanreview.mit.edu/article/why-the-highest-price-isnt-the-best-price/

Anderson, Patrick et al. "Price elasticity of demand." 1997, https://scholar.harvard.edu/files/alada/files/price_elasticity_of_demand_handout.pdf

Anthony, Scott, "Kodak's Downfall Wasn't About Technology," *Harvard Business Review*, 24 Apr. 2017, https://hbr.org/2016/07/kodaks-downfall-wasnt-about-technology

Basu, Dev. "Inbound Marketing: The Customer Finds You." *The Globe and Mail*, Special to The Globe and Mail, 11 July 2012, www.theglobeandmail.com/report-on-business/small-business/sb-marketing/inbound-marketing-the-customer-finds-you/article4258852/

Best, Roger J. *Market- Based Management*. Pearson, 2014.

Bezos, Jeff. "2016 Letter to Shareholders," https://www.amazon.com/p/feature/z609g6sysxur57t

Biyani, Gagan. "The Difference Between Growth Hacking and Marketing." *The Next Web*, 11 Apr. 2016, https://thenextweb.com/insider/2013/05/05/the-actual-difference-between-growth-hacking-and-marketing-explained/

Boehm, Martin. "Pricing Strategy." *Coursera*, Mar. 2018, www.coursera.org/learn/pricing-strategy

Brooks, David. *The Road to Character*. Random House New York, 2015.

Brooks, David. *The Social Animal: The Hidden Sources of Love*. Random House Trade Paperbacks, 2012.

Cagan, Marty. "Product Success." *Silicon Valley Product Group*, 30 Nov. 2016, https://svpg.com/product-success/

Cagan, Marty. "The Root Cause of Product Failure - Marty Cagan, at USI." *YouTube*, 18 July 2016, www.youtube.com/watch?v=jVbVEdF75PE&t=578s

Cooper, Robert G., and Scott J. Edgett. *Lean, Rapid, and Profitable New Product Development*. Product Development Institute, 2010.

Cooper, Robert. "Stage-Gate and Agile Development: Debunking the Myths." *Stage-Gate and Agile Development: Debunking the Myths | Stage-Gate International*, www.stage-gate.com/resources_stage-gate_agile.php

den Holder, Greetje. "Here Is What Growth Hacking Is NOT." *BudgetVertalingOnline*, 29 Nov. 2016, http://budgetvertalingonline.nl/business/what-growth-hacking-is-not/

Dholakia, Utpal M. "A Quick Guide to Value-Based Pricing." *Harvard Business Review*, 9 Aug. 2016, https://hbr.org/2016/08/a-quick-guide-to-value-based-pricing

Eriksson, Martin. "Using The Kano Model To Prioritize Product Development." *Mind the Product*, 4 July 2017, www.mindtheproduct.com/2013/07/using-the-kano-model-to-prioritize-product-development/

Ewalt, David M. *Of Dice and Men: The Story of Dungeons & Dragons and the People Who Play It.* Scribner, 2014.

Freitas, João. "Learning Center." *The Complete Guide to Inbound Marketing*, Mar. 2018, www.mezzolab.com/en/blog/cycle_of_inbound_marketing

Gorchels, Linda. *The Product Manager's Handbook.* McGraw-Hill, 2012.

Greylock Partners, "Rethink transportation safety with Reid Hoffman and Nauto CEO Stefan Heck," *Greymatter*, December 2017 https://soundcloud.com/greylock-partners/rethinking-transportation-safety

Hambrick, Donald C., and James W. Fredrickson. "Are You Sure You Have a Strategy?" *Academy of Management Executive*, vol. 19, no. 4, 2005, pp. 51–62., doi:10.5465/ame.2005.19417907.

Heath, Chip, and Dan Heath. *Decisive: How to Make Better Choices in Life and Work.* Random House Business, 2014.

Jahandarpour, Ehsan. "4 Growth Hacking Strategies That Work Like Magic." *Entrepreneur*, 27 June 2016, www.entrepreneur.com/article/276641

Kahneman, Daniel. *Thinking, Fast and Slow.* Farrar, Straus and Giroux, 2015.

Kano, Noriaki, et al. "Attractive Quality and Must-be Quality." Journal of the Japanese Society for Quality Control (in Japanese), April 1984.

Kaplan, Steven et al. "Which CEO Characteristics and Abilities Matter?" Swedish Institute for Financial Research Conference on Economics of the Private Equity Market, July 2008, http://faculty.chicagobooth.edu/steven.kaplan/research/kks.pdf

Klau, Rick. "Startup Lab Workshop: How Google Sets Goals: OKRs." *YouTube*, 14 May 2013, www.youtube.com/watch?v=mJB83EZtAjc

Korosec, Kirsten. "Self-Driving Cars: Investors Pour Millions Into Tech Startup Nauto."*Fortune*, 19 July 2017, http://fortune.com/2017/07/19/nauto-self-driving-cars-autonomous-vehicles/

Kotler, Philip. *Marketing Management: Analysis, Planning, Implementation, and Control.* Prentice-Hall, 2003.

LinkedIn. "About LinkedIn." *LinkedIn Newsroom*, Mar. 2018, www.press.linkedin.com/about-linkedin

LinkedIn. "Sign Up." Mar. 2018, www.linkedin.com

Loehr, James E., and Tony Schwartz. *The Power of Full Engagement: Managing Energy, Not Time, Is the Key to High Performance and Personal Renewal.* Free Press, 2005.

Lucas, Henry C. *The Search for Survival: Lessons from Disruptive Technologies.* Praeger, 2012.

Markoff, John. "Robot Cars Can't Count on Us in an Emergency." *The New York Times*, The New York Times, 7 June 2017, www.nytimes.com/2017/06/07/technology/google-self-driving-cars-handoff-problem.html?mcubz=1&_r=0

Marn, Michael V., et al. "Pricing New Products." *McKinsey & Company*, Mar. 2018, www.mckinsey.com/business-functions/marketing-and-sales/our-insights/pricing-new-products

Mironov, Rich. "A VP Product's Checklist." *Rich Mironov's Product Bytes*, 26 Jan. 2016, www.mironov.com/vppm-list/

Mironov, Rich. "Hearing About Accounts, Listening for Segments." *Rich Mironov's Product Bytes*, 27 Aug. 2017, www.mironov.com/segments/

Mironov, Rich. "Selling vs. Learning." *Rich Mironov's Product Bytes*, 19 Jan. 2017, www.mironov.com/learning/

O'Kelley, Luke. "B2B Marketing Buzzwords: Growth Hacking Vs. Inbound Marketing." *MLT Creative*, Luke O'Kelley Https://Www.mltcreative.com/Wp-Content/Uploads/2013/04/MLT_Creative_logo.Png, 4 Dec. 2015, www.mltcreative.com/blog/b2b-marketing-buzzwords-growth-hacking-vs-inbound-marketing/

Osterwalder, Alexander, et al. *Value Proposition Design: How to Create Products and Services Customers Want.* Wiley, 2015.

Parr, Sam. "How Udemy Found Their First 1,000 Instructors... Tips For Building a Marketplace with Gagan Biyani." *The Hustle,* 5 June 2015, https://thehustle.co/build-marketplace-gagan-biyani-founder-udemy-sprig

Prescott, Bill. "Business Sense: In-Bound Marketing." *Times-Standard,* 2012, www.times-standard.com/article/zz/20120205/NEWS/120209434

Rekhi, Sachin. "The Art of Product Management with Sachin Rekhi (ENG'05 W'05)." *YouTube,* 20 May 2016, www.youtube.com/watch?v=huTSPanUlQM&t=844s

Schwartz, Tony, et al. *The Way We're Working Isn't Working: The Four Forgotten Needs That Energize Great Performance.* Free Press, 2010.

Seba, Tony. *Rethinking Transportation 2020-2030.* 2017, https://tonyseba.com/portfolio-item/rethinking-transportation-2020-2030/

Semick, Jim. "Guide to Product Roadmaps." *Product Roadmap Book,* Mar. 2018, www.productplan.com/lp/product-roadmap-book/

Sims, Peter. *Little Bets: How Big Ideas Emerge from Small Discoveries.* Random House Business, 2012.

SpaceX. "Careers." *SpaceX,* February 2018, www.spacex.com/careers

Tiner, Colleen. "Use the Market to Gain Credibility." *Pragmatic Marketing,* 16 Apr. 2013, www.pragmaticmarketing.com/resources/articles/use-the-market-to-gain-credibility

Usborne, David. "The Moment It All Went Wrong for Kodak." *The Independent,* Independent Digital News and Media, 20 Jan. 2012, www.independent.co.uk/news/business/analysis-and-features/the-moment-it-all-went-wrong-for-kodak-6292212.html

Watkins, Michael. *The First 90 Days: Proven Strategies for Getting up to Speed Faster and Smarter.* Harvard Business Review Press, 2013.

Wikimedia. "Vision." *Wikimedia Foundation,* Feb. 2018, www.wikimediafoundation.org/wiki/Vision

ABOUT THE AUTHOR

Todd Birzer helps product managers and their teams become more strategic—empowering them to develop products that delight customers, generate sustainable competitive advantage, and drive long-term profitability.

Working as a product management consultant, teacher, and coach, Todd helps product managers:

- Gain a deeper understanding of the articulated and unarticulated needs of customers
- Develop long-term product strategies for customer delight and competitive advantage
- Run an effective discovery and delivery product development process
- Systematically find growth and profitability for a company's products

Todd has an MBA from Wharton, at the University of Pennsylvania.

If you would like product management templates associated with this book, or otherwise would like help with your product management work, you can reach out to Todd through LinkedIn (www.linkedin.com/in/toddbirzer) or via email (todd@kevolve.com).

Printed in Great Britain
by Amazon

66597001R00106